COYOTE SPEAKS

WONDERS OF THE NATIVE AMERICAN WORLD

COYOTE SPEAKS

WONDERS OF THE NATIVE AMERICAN WORLD

Ari Berk & Carolyn Dunn

ABRAMS BOOKS FOR YOUNG READERS
NEW YORK

A NOTE ON ART & TEXT

Where petroglyphs appear without credit (such as on this page) they are drawn by Ari Berk, from actual rock drawings. In respect to each artwork in this book, every attempt has been made to supply the date of creation and the name of the associated tribe or region. If a story has a known title, it is provided. Under the title, the relevant tribe is named in parentheses, or it is given just prior to the story.

Library of Congress Cataloging-in-Publication Data

Berk, Ari.
Coyote speaks : wonders of the Native American world / by Ari Berk and Carolyn Dunn.
p. cm.
Includes bibliographical references.
ISBN-13: 978-0-8109-9372-3 (hardcover w/jacket)
ISBN-10: 0-8109-9372-4 (hardcover w/jacket)
1. Indians of North America—Folklore. 2. Indian mythology—North America—Juvenile literature. 3. Indians of North America—Social life and customs—Juvenile literature. I. Dunn, Carolyn, 1965–II. Title.

E98.F6B49 2008
398.2089'97—dc22
2006032833

Text copyright © 2008 Ari Berk and Carolyn Dunn
For illustration credits please see page 154.

Book design by Maria T. Middleton

Published in 2008 by Abrams Books for Young Readers,
an imprint of Harry N. Abrams, Inc.

Printed and bound in China
10 9 8 7 6 5 4 3 2 1

HNA
harry n. abrams, inc.
a subsidiary of La Martinière Groupe
115 West 18th Street
New York, NY 10011
www.hnabooks.com

This book is dedicated to the memory of my grandparents,
Morton and Nellie Gilford, and Alexander and Clarice Berk.
—A. B.

For the storytellers whose words grace this book: the stories are alive
and will continue; with love and thanks to my grandparents and their
great-grandchildren.
—C. D.

✣ ✣ ✣

Contents

COYOTE SPEAKS

WONDERS OF THE NATIVE AMERICAN WORLD

Here, the Earth Is Brown

Skin sheds dry tears
in the midst of burning sky
where grief lives,
walking among us
like the end of beauty.
A wavering soul, Coyote
wandered upon this scorched land,
like a cricket across
an asphalt highway
in midday miles
of sweltering air.
We talk a good song,
wishing for light and
stars to speak our
names.
Endless,
faceless,
the stories weave themselves
into a seamless
passage of slow,
burning time.
Across a living sea
the land breathes the
songs of a
wandering westering soul,
a brown story told in red
a whisper upon the breath
of every living thing.
Dancing a song
from a distant

place of memory, of myth,
we move in a circle,
holding court with
our mouths,
our brown bodies painted red,
pink shells and
sky-blue pieces of
turquoise, we melt,
fade away into the
color of a distant star
where wandering is alive.
The call to this land
keeps us moving,
dancing
and this way
will be known
forever,
this dance of memory,
of myth and renewal,
and remembrance of
the place
where footsteps
and song
led us dancing,
and wandering through
the dark and dry earth.
Coyote speaks, singing a charm song
and we, transfixed,
can only listen.

OPPOSITE: Inuit stone sculpture, called an *inuksuk*, Hudson Bay, Alaska. Stone cairns, or man-made piles of stones, such as this were used over much of the North for driving caribou, which mistook them for hunters. They were also used as landmarks to aid winter travelers in finding their way across a frozen landscape.

This Is Yo Luck by L. Frank (Tongva/Ajachumen), 1995.

"Ah to dah."

Everything fits together.

(Cherokee)

IMAGINE:

✳ a time when there was only a thin line between the realms of humans and animals, and they could speak to each other and share their knowledge, or transform from one into the other through magic.

✳ a world where Coyote makes the heavens by holding all the stars in a blanket and then throwing them into the sky, where they become the constellations that we still see today.

✳ a land where people emerged into this world by growing like corn from beneath the ground.

✳ ancient objects, amazing journeys, mysterious symbols, and magical stories.

Now imagine that all these things exist, for in Native America, they do.

The Ballgame Between the Birds and the Animals
(Cherokee)

It has been said that one time, the animals challenged the birds to a stickball game, and the birds accepted. The dance grounds were by the river and the People were dancing. It was there the animals met to discuss their game. Yona, the bear, was the head of the animal team; he was very strong, and could beat back anyone who got in his way. All along the way to the stickball game, he was showing his strength by tossing logs and boulders into the air. "I'll toss the birds from the eastern shore to the western," Yona bragged to anyone who could hear. Dagasi, the turtle, was a huge turtle, and his shell was so hard, not even the heaviest blow to him would hurt. "I'll crush the next bird who gets close to me with my hard shell," he boasted to all around him. Awi, the great deer, was so fast she could outrun anyone around her. "I can outrun any bird on wings," she insisted. The animals were indeed a great team.

The birds had Wahali, the eagle, as their leader. Her vision was clear and strong. Tawodi, the hawk, had speed in flight that could match any distance covered twice as fast as most animals. Although they were swift and strong, the birds were still a little worried about the game. In the trees above the dance grounds, all the birds were nervously pruning their feathers and waiting for the captain to give the word. All of a sudden, there came two little things hardly bigger than field mice, and they climbed up the tree where Wahali, the eagle, was sitting. They asked to join in the game. She looked at them, and seeing that they were four-legged, asked why they didn't go down to the animal team. They said they had, but the animals laughed, and made fun of them, because they were so small. Wahali felt sorry for them, so she took the two little things to the others.

But these new animals had no wings. Wahali, Tawodi, and the others consulted, and finally decided to make some wings for the little ones. They tried for a very long time to think of a solution, when finally someone thought about the drum they had used in the dance. The head was made of groundhog skin. Maybe they could take off a corner of the leather and make some wings. They took two pieces from the drumhead and cut them into wing shapes and stretched them with cane splints and fastened them to the front legs of one of the little animals.

This is how Tlameha, the bat, came to be.

They threw the ball to him and told him to catch it. He darted and circled about, and always kept the ball in the air and never let it hit the ground. The birds soon felt that he would be one of their best players.

Now they figured they'd better fix the other poor animal, but they had no more leather to make wings. Somebody thought of stretching his skin, the way the leather had been stretched on the drum. Two large birds took hold of each side of him with their strong beaks, and pulled at his fur for several minutes. They managed to stretch the skin between his front and back legs, until they had Tewa, the squirrel. To see how well he could play, the captain threw the ball up in the air, and Tewa leaped off the limb, caught it in his teeth, and carried it through the air until he reached another tree, far, far away.

When both sides were ready, the signal was given and the game began. Almost at the very first, Tewa caught the ball and carried it to a tree, from which he threw it to the other birds. They kept it in the air for a very long time, but it finally dropped. Yona, the bear, rushed to grab it, but Tlutlu, the martin, darted after it and threw it to Tlameha. By his dodging and circling, the bat kept it out of the way of even Awi, until Tlameha finally threw it to the pole and won the game for the birds.

Yona and Dagasi, who had bragged about how good they were and what they would do to the birds, never even got a chance to play. For saving the ball when it dropped, the birds gave Tlutlu a beautiful gourd in which he could build his nest. Today, he still has it.

Woodpecker gorget (a kind of necklace), Mississippian culture, Tennessee, early eleventh century. In this representation, the sun is encircled by the four directions of the wind and framed by the crested woodpeckers, which are a sign of a call to war. As in the story, birds play an important role in early Mississippian art, representing elemental forces.

Among the many tribes of Native Americans, these stories (like the Cherokee one told at the beginning of this chapter) are still told, ancient objects are kept, and beautiful art is still made. These stories and objects are the containers of powerful traditions, many of which have been remembered for thousands of years. Though much has changed since ancient times, many of the old traditions are still practiced and many of the old stories are as meaningful today as they were a thousand years ago.

It is important to remember that there are more than five hundred distinct Native American tribes, with as many languages and customs. When we speak about Native Americans, we must remember these differences between tribes. Along with language and cultural diversity, such as traditions, beliefs, stories, and songs, many Native American societies have changed with the times, while still cherishing a strong relationship with their past and the ways of their ancestors. The old stories and ancient beliefs have always been the most important to preserve, because they speak of origins, magic, delight, and wisdom. By telling these stories and holding true to their beliefs, many Native Americans stay deeply connected to their past and to the living world around them.

While these beliefs may be very different from those practiced by your family (beliefs differ from tribe to tribe as well), they are no less true, and it is necessary to respect them. These are living traditions—stories that are still being told, ceremonies still being enacted—all handed down from generation to generation. When we speak of Native American peoples and listen to their stories, we must be respectful and remember that it is through their stories and traditions that Native peoples have preserved their culture through many hardships. Through language they have come to understand the world around them. Stories explain their surroundings as well as relationships to family and friends. Native peoples also use stories to communicate traditional knowledge (dances, ceremonies, songs, and beliefs that are passed down), as well as to remember the past and to honor the present. When we walk the lands of these stories in our imaginations, it is vital to understand that we are guests and need to tread softly.

OPPOSITE: Cliff Palace, Mesa Verde, Colorado, twelfth century. Underground ceremonial chambers, called *kivas*, are an important part of origin myths among Southwestern native cultures because the act of climbing out of a *kiva* re-creates mythic emergence from the Lower World into this one.

Booger mask. Made of a hornet nest, used to drive away illness. Cherokee, ca. 1930.

CHAPTER ONE

Medicine People
Walkers Between the Worlds

Coyote Madonna

Wandering
at night
under stars
and a moon
of time in
distant skies
and stars of life.
At night she whispers a prayer
and the world falls silent.
Light dots the landscape
reflecting stars off the black ocean sky
and her voice pares away
at the noise
like the knife at her belt.
Her eyes are stars and a blessing.
Once the quiet stills, she moves across hills
across sage
chaparral

and wild alata
singing a song that keeps sleep
at the place behind our eyes.
The quiet keeps us down
but for her the silence is music,
    a song of
heart and memory
like stars that shine her way
light across a desert plain.
Lifting her ears, they move forward, back,
    close to her head.
She sniffs the ground
and on wings of sand and glass
takes flight
toward the cry of someone's child
    upon the wind.
Bring them home, distant stars lit
    on your path

and wisdom
of the ancestors
her paws stretch like wings
to carry them home.
Each finds a home close to her heart.

The color
of the sky before sunrise
and moonset
summons the
Silence home.
The sounds of city breath and brokenness
that brings
us back from our dreams.
From her mouth
come our voices

waking, rising,
they drift over hills and wild alata,
tobacco,
sagebrush, chaparral and remnants of real
and imaginary places.
Taking the loss
within her wings she flies home,
rooting the lost ones to her breasts.
Flying unladen now
they move across
the shining sky
the in-betweens and the lost ones
have found their home
as the sun rises,
giving voice back to the ones who have none.

OPPOSITE: Navajo medicine rattle with buffalo tail, mountain lion fur, and lightning designs. Used in healing ceremonies from mid-to-late twentieth century.

One day, near Chinle . . .

. . . There was a man who had accidentally killed a rattlesnake. This was a terrible thing. Snakes are powerful creatures and are related to the thunder and lightning. They are a link between earth and sky. Killing snakes was forbidden. So this man who killed the snake got sick. Weeks passed and he did not improve. His family sent for a "singer," a medicine man.

The night for the ceremony came and the stars began their dance. The medicine man and his helpers used colored sand to make intricate designs on the dirt floor of the family's hogan. Gods, animals, thunder creatures, rainbows, arrows, and many other powerful objects and beings were painted. When the painting was finished, the medicine man, or *hataalii* ("chanter" in the Navajo language), took his rattle and began to sing. The songs were very special and they told an ancient story. As the *hataalii* chanted, the sick man was led onto the painting. As the ancient stories were sung, the gods and spirits listened; the sick man *became* the man in the story. The story-song carried him back in time, to the moment when Creation first occurred. Now the sick man was in two worlds at once, or between the worlds. He became part of the One Story that has been told since the earliest time. He remembered that he has always been a part of the One Story.

The *hataalii* sang about the power of snakes, and how to heal someone who has been bitten, or who has killed one. The singing went on long into the night, and as the story ended and the People in the story were healed, so the man sitting on the sand painting knew that he, too, had been healed. The singing of the story, the magic of Winds, Thunder, and Lightning restored him.

"We are all part of the ancient stories," said the *hataalii*. "What our ancestors have lived, we live. As they were healed by magic, so can we be healed, if we remember the stories and tell them right."

The stars ended their dance. The singing had taken all night and the sun was rising outside the hogan. Food was prepared. A feast was held.

This story is typical of how medicine men and women practice their doctoring among the Navajo, or Diné, people. But every tribe has its own medicine people or medicine societies. Medicine people are similar to doctors . . . they heal the sick within the community and are very important to the health of the tribe. Not only do they heal the sick, but they help with hunting, and they also keep in memory the stories and traditions of the People. The medicine people carry the knowledge of ceremonies that assist the People in bringing healing to the community. Ceremonies remind communities of their relationship to the land, to one another, and to the spirits that surround them. Ceremonies are part of a rich tradition of words and songs that keep communities together—in prayer and in play—in day-to-day life.

Most important, medicine people know the land. They remember the names of every hill and stream. They keep the stories of everything in the landscape, for every place has a story surrounding it. They can interpret the causes of illness and know the healing properties of plants and herbs—which plants to use for certain conditions, which ceremonies are needed during certain seasons of the year. Their roles are very important in Native traditions, and many Native people look to the medicine men and women for health and healing within their communities.

Many non-Indian doctors today are beginning to use other kinds of medicine in their practices. The use of herbs, and other "alternative" medicines are really only a return to what medicine people have always known: The body and the mind must be treated together. The medicine man or woman uses stories, healing plants, stones, special objects, and music to help heal the sick. In Native American medicine, the whole *person* is treated, not only the body.

LEFT: Navajo bull roarer. A ritual object used when the *hataalii*, the medicine man, is communicating with spirits.

OPPOSITE: Bone and inlaid-abalone soul catcher, Tlingit, Northwest coast. The soul catcher was the most important item used by shamans during curing ceremonies. When sickness was believed to be the result of the soul leaving the body, a shaman was hired to search for the errant soul, which he enticed to enter his soul catcher. Securely sealed within, the soul could be carried back to the patient.

ANGALQUK OF THE NORTH

In the cold lands of the North a kind of medicine person, now often called a shaman (though that word comes from Siberia, not Native America), is responsible for healing the sick, making medicine for the hunt, using magic to affect the weather, and communicating between the human world and the realm of spirits. Among the Inuit (sometimes called Eskimo), this person is known as an *angalquk*, or "one who commands respect," and is usually a man, though women sometimes occupy this role. Some of their power comes from remembering a powerful dream they might have had. People who became very sick and had visions or dreams might become an *angalquk* if they survived. That person would become the apprentice or student of an older shaman, and in that way come to learn about magic, spirits, and healing. But to become an *angalquk* is not usually thought of as a good thing. The responsibility of the *angalquk* is very great, and sometimes there is danger involved in these healing practices, in communicating with spirits and animals, and in traveling into the Otherworld (the realm of gods, spirits, and ancestors) to help people. Such responsibility can be very physically and emotionally difficult. Knowing this, parents would tell their children not to remember the shaman's songs for fear that the child might obtain some of the shaman's power and have to become an *angalquk* too.

From the earliest times, when people became ill, it was believed that they had lost a part of their soul, part of that special power or spirit that makes them who they are. This could happen in many different ways: by offending animals, spirits, or ancestors; through injury; or by breaking a tribal rule or custom. When this kind of sickness happened, it would be the *angalquk*'s job to follow the spirit or soul of the sick person into the Otherworld and bring it back. This often meant that the *angalquk* would have to undergo physically difficult ceremonies, such as dancing and singing for many hours or days at a time, and perhaps have to battle or subdue frightening spirits in order to heal the patient. It was never an easy job, but the *angalquk*, like all medicine people in all tribes, has special skills and tools to help him in his work.

HELPING SPIRITS

As is common among medicine people of all tribes for the performance of important work, the *angalquk* relies very heavily on the assistance he or she is given by "helping spirits." These take many different forms, and each *angalquk* will have a different group of helping spirits that work with him. Sometimes they take the form of animals—or several animals combined into one, making a strange and powerful creature known only to the *angalquk*. Helping spirits may also be people once known to the medicine person who, now deceased, help him from the spirit world. Whatever their form, these helping spirits act as guides and protectors as well as giving valuable wisdom and insight to the medicine person that they work with. Here, Otaq, a young man of the Polar Inuit, describes his helpers and the beginning of his work as an *angalquk*:

Shaman's charms, Tsimshian, Northwest coast, nineteenth century. During curing rites, in a trance, Tsimshian shamans used these amulets, representing the creatures from which they derived powers, to retrieve the spirit of a patient. Even small objects contain great power.

WHEN I SAW THE HILL SPIRITS again a great dog was running after them, a parti-colored dog: it, too, became a helping spirit . . . . I revealed myself as a magician. And I helped many who were ill. My Helping Spirits know my thoughts and my will, and they help me when I give them commands.

MAGICAL MUSIC

Anyone who loves music knows how powerful it can be. Music can alter our feelings, calling up sadness and joy, sometimes both in the same song. Some music has the power to relax us, other kinds can excite us, make us dance or want to sing. Music, drumming, singing, and the power of rhythms and beats can affect us (and our moods and health) very deeply. Even our heartbeats make a kind of music, so perhaps we can think of ourselves as instruments, always producing rhythm and always capable of being powerfully affected by the music we make or hear. Belief in the power of music is present in every Native American tribe. As in the North, southern tribes like the Choctaw know that the magic of music helps those who still sing with strong voices. Those songs are stories. Some of them are still being sung and told.

That Painted Horse
(Choctaw)

A group of men were looking to start trouble with their enemies, being that's how men are. They had noticed that their enemies always looked so fine on their big, beautiful horses with eyes seemingly on fire. The enemies seemed to ride taller and stronger than the men, and the men began to talk amongst themselves. "Our enemies always seem so brave and strong on those horses! We need to get some of those horses ourselves so we can have the upper hand on those others."

Now the men had tried before to take their enemies' horses, but they weren't successful. Every time the men came upon the horse camp of their enemies, the horses and the enemies were long gone. The enemies always seemed to know exactly the men's thoughts and actions before even they did. The enemies always seemed to know when they were coming, and often moved their camp in advance of the men's attacks.

One of the men, Honokee, the whirlwind, was riding one day and came to a beautiful open meadow at the edge of a river. He was thirsty, and had bent down at the river's edge to take a sip of water when he spied a beautiful painted horse with strong chestnut and white colors. He stayed quiet in the grass and watched the horse move along the water, then back into the tall grass from where she came. Silently, Honokee padded along a trail behind the horse and before long came to a place where there were many large rocks.

Behind the rocks, many horses of all colors and sizes grazed peacefully. How beautiful they were! Horses of many colors with handprints stamped upon them—all colors of the red sky at dawn, the pale of early morning, and the blackest of night. Honokee had found the enemies' camp!

Carefully he slipped away from the horses and returned to his sister, Ipanche Falaya, who was a medicine doctor. Honokee knew that his sister had strong, powerful magic that would help him in his quest to surprise the enemy and win some horses for the men.

"Ipanche Falaya, *ahn teek*, I need your help. You know that I love you and I love our people, and that the horses of our enemies will make us stronger and faster, and I seek to honor you and our family by gifting many horses. *Ahn teek*, I need you. Give me a charm to help me be steadfast and silent, to gather horses from the camp of our enemies and bring them safely to our clan, our nation, our people."

Ipanche Falaya loved her brother, and he was a good man. She knew just what type of magic he needed: words that had a life of their own to aid her brother in his hunting skills.

The medicine doctor smiled and said, "I'll give you a song that will show both your enemies and their horses that you mean business."

Honokee, under the cover of darkness, came to his enemies' camp. Near the camp were the horses he had seen so very recently. This time, his enemies slept there also.

Honokee sang the song his sister Ipanche Falaya had given him:

Isoba besoua mako,
Ogla hey chey hunk o pag mah,
Ogla hey chey hunk o pag mah,
Ogla hush na to ma chey
Hush na to ma chey.

Shaman's seal-hide drum, Inuit, Alaska. In many tribes, the power of song is often accentuated by the beat of the drum, reflective of the heartbeat of the earth.

Meaning:
That painted horse over there,
What will all of you do,
Oh what will you all do
When
We steal it?

Startled, the enemies awoke to find their horses running away in a cloud of red dirt and mud. They could hear the sound of hooves punching into the soft earth, but could see nothing, so great was their confusion.

Honokee came back home, painted horses following him. The tallest and most beautiful he gave to his sister, Ipanche Falaya, for her medicine was very powerful indeed. ☀

Music is a very important part of most Native American ceremonies. Among the Inuit, drums are called *qilaut,* or "that which helps call up the spirits," while among the Anishinabe, or Ojibwe, people, the word *omiigiwen* refers to the giving of a gift of friendship that usually takes the form of a drum. Drums are alive and symbolize the tribal nation's heartbeat. Considered sacred ritual objects, drums are played by medicine people to help them enter into a state of mind where they can travel in the spirit world and heal the patient. The powerful beat of the drum helps the medicine people focus their strength and conjure helpful spirits who will aid them. In this trance state—which, depending upon the ceremony and the individual medicine person, could be enacted through shaking, crying, dancing, or a prolonged silence—the medicine person might travel to the moon, far beyond the hills, or beneath the sea to consult with powerful spirits. Rattles, too, are used to help diagnose illness or to frighten harmful spirits.

Medicine people have magic songs to help them also. The words of the songs are often kept secret, for it is believed that if someone else learns a particular medicine person's song, that song's power could be lessened. These songs are considered personal possessions and make up part of an individual medicine person's wealth, along with his material belongings. Complete and total faith in the power of words is an important

part of what gives each medicine person's songs and spells their ability to heal, affect the weather, and work magic.

PIECES OF POWER

Along with music and words, special objects are found or made to help the medicine people in their work. All tribes make use of charms and fetishes—stones, feathers, a carving, a piece of bone, twisted twigs— all are pieces of a spell that makes up the medicine person's ability to do the work of helping others, of keeping balance between this world and the others.

Such objects could be hung on belts, made into necklaces, or kept in special pouches, bags, or bundles. Each small object—an elk tooth, for example— represents animal allies, or a place the medicine person had been, or something that might have been given to him by the spirits or was found or gotten in a special way. These objects help to strengthen the medicine person's power. Charms are important not only because they contain power in and of themselves, but because they are part of the medicine person's spiritual memory—his or her ability to use traditions and experiences to bring about change or healing through associative magic—rituals that strengthen connections between humans and the natural and spiritual worlds around them.

The power of charms is around us all the time, though we might not know it. Think of things you have collected, or that make you feel safe or something you picked up that felt good in your hand: a stone, a

TOP: Part of a Haida shaman's gear included a necklace from which various bone and ivory charms were suspended. Haida, Queen Charlotte Islands.

BOTTOM: "Rock medicine" would have been kept inside medicine bundles that were opened at the first sound of thunder in spring and just before the onset of winter. Crow, northern Plains.

beloved toy, a wind-smoothed branch you found below an ancient tree, a gift from your grandmother that was a gift from her grandmother. These kinds of objects have a subtle kind of magic. They remind us of special times, events, or places. By using such objects to remind us of the good things in our lives, we can help ourselves feel better.

MEDICINE SOCIETIES AND PRIESTS

Some tribes—like those of the Plains or in the North—have medicine men or shamans, individuals who use their knowledge and powers to help and heal the tribe. Shamans and medicine men and women can usually (but not always) be found among tribes who rely mostly on hunting for their food.

Medicine bundle belonging to the Weasel chapter of the Crow Tobacco Society, late nineteenth century. During ceremonies the bundle was opened and women danced with the weasel skins to obtain supernatural power that ensured the fertility of the sacred tobacco and, therefore, the fertility and growth of the Crow tribe as a whole. Bags such as this are used to store rituals, stories, and tribal histories, and are themselves objects of great reverence.

Other tribes—like the Pueblos (Hopi, Zuni, Laguna, Zia, Taos, Jemez and others) and the Iroquois, or Haudenosaunee (People of the Long House)—depend on the knowledge of medicine societies. Traditionally agricultural tribes like these rely on planting and harvesting for most of their foods. Among these people, organization of the community at large is vitally important. A strong community is needed to tend the fields and ensure the health of the harvest. Because of the importance of community, group cooperation, and communal activities, the keepers of tradition in these cultures tend to be groups also. Medicine power would then be held by an organization, or medicine society, and not usually by an individual. There are many different kinds of societies. Some are healing societies. Others are made up of astronomers. Some are made up of warriors and hunters. Each medicine society has specific jobs to do in helping the community survive.

THE POWER OF THE MASK: FALSE-FACE SOCIETIES OF THE HAUDENOSAUNEE

The Haudenosaunee of the Northeast tell of a curious creature who had its home on a gigantic rock. It had long hair, so long that the hair flowed down all over the rock. Like many spirits with strange or ugly appearances, this one could inflict illness or send disease among the People. By capturing the images of these creatures in masks, the Iroquois people of the False-Face Society controlled the power of these spirits and used it for good and for healing.

The masks were made in a special way, and it was important to get the wood from a living basswood tree. The mask was carved into the trunk, and tobacco was offered to the Tree Spirit, asking forgiveness for damaging it. Tobacco smoke was blown all around the tree—among the branches, among the roots—and special carving songs were sung. Even the finished mask required special treatment. It was, after all, a living thing, a creation of power. Tobacco bags were tied to it, and it was not put away in a trunk or box for fear of offending the spirit of the mask.

All members of the False-Face Society owned such masks, and there were many different styles. The healing ceremonies were usually performed in the beginning of each year. The False-Face doctor would spread ashes on the patients to help cure them. Other ceremonies, such as purifying houses, were performed in the spring and fall, or as needed. After the ceremonies, great feasts were held to celebrate the blessings brought about by the False-Face spirits.

HOPI SNAKE DANCE

The Snake Dance of the Hopi tribe in Arizona is held in August of every other year. This is a sixteen-day ceremony, believed to once have been practiced by all the Rio Grande Pueblo tribes. Today it survives only among the Hopi.

The ceremony ritually shows the journey of a young man who goes in search of the source of a river. He eventually encounters the Great Snake, who rules all the waters of the world from his *kiva* (an underground ceremonial chamber). The young man is accepted into the snake clan and marries a girl who has been transformed into a snake. Because of this marriage (which is a powerful symbol of the linking of earth—the young man—and the lightning in the sky—the snake-girl), the youth is given snake medicine and allowed to share its wisdom and power among his own people.

The first four days of the ceremony (eight days before the public dance) are spent gathering the snakes. Men of the Snake and Antelope Societies search the six directions of the desert below the mesa and bring back as many snakes as they can find to the *kiva* for washing and blessing. As symbols of the rain spirits, the snakes are treated very carefully in a sacred manner and blessed with cornmeal.

Toward evening on the eighth day, the Snake dancers and Antelope dancers appear in a plaza, facing each other. The sound of gourd rattles, imitating the noise of a giant rattlesnake, can be heard.

The Antelope men carry cornstalks in their mouths and move around the plaza. The cornstalk is handled as though it is a serpent. This action is used to emphasize the relationship between the corn and the rain. The dance calls rain so that the corn will grow.

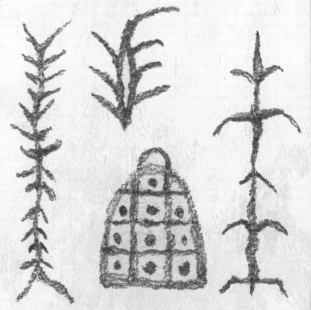

RIGHT: Petroglyph depictions of corn, Four Corners region, south-western United States. Petroglyphs were carved on rock. The spirit world is often represented on rocks and stones by medicine people.

OPPOSITE, TOP: Corn-husk mask.

OPPOSITE, BOTTOM: False-Face mask, used as a powerful element in ceremonies of the False-Face medicine society to help appease spirits. Haudenosaunee (Iroquois), Northeast woodlands.

So the snake, as a symbol of lightning and the sky, is very important to the health of the crops. If the snake is treated well, rain will come.

The next day, there is more dancing, but now it is the Snake Priests who dance, and instead of cornstalks, they dance with real snakes in their mouths. It is believed that only the very pure in heart and mind can dance with this sacred creature in his mouth. They hold the snakes very carefully so as not to hurt them. After each snake has been danced around the plaza, it is placed within a circle of sacred cornmeal. Then, suddenly, the snakes are picked up by men who run down the mesas to return the animals to the desert, where they are to act as messengers who will carry the Hopi's prayers for rain to the rain spirits.

As the snakes slide away behind the mesa, clouds are gathering. The People know that soon the rains will come and the corn will grow.

A CONTINUING TRADITION

All tribes have medicine people, or medicine societies. These important people are keepers of tradition and help bridge the gap between the world of ordinary men and women, and the world of spirits, ancestors, and gods. Some work alone, calling upon powerful helping spirits to diagnose illness and heal the sick; some paint magic images with sand and sing health back into their patients; others work together in medicine societies, dancing for rain and bringing blessings upon the crops and all the People of their tribe. Sometimes, the advice given by medicine people can be very simple:

ABOVE: Hopi Cloud Maiden *kachina*. As spirits of the invisible life forces, *kachinas* are represented in masked dances and ceremonies from the winter solstice until July, bringing rain for spring crops. *Kachina* dolls are given to children to teach them about the Hopi spirit world.

OPPOSITE, TOP: Tiny fiber-and-bone figurines from Hogup Cave, Utah, late third century. People are often encouraged by spiritual leaders to leave offerings such as these.

OPPOSITE, BOTTOM: Petroglyph, Bighorn Basin, Wyoming. People of power are frequently depicted in rock art.

HERE WERE THE OLD MAN'S words: To get rid of anger or bad feelings, take a small stick and hold it tightly in your hand; squeeze it as hard as you can. Now take this object to a place of moving water, a stream or river. Place the stick upon the current and watch it move away from you. Watch until it drifts from sight. When this is done, your anger or bad feelings will be gone.

Medicine people still practice their craft, and medicine societies are still strong. Though they are rarer than in early days, medicine people still live and work among rural Native American communities. Others live in cities. All things change over time, and Native American communities have changed also. Yet the need for people with healing gifts has endured, even in our modern age of great medical advances. The stress of living in a modern, industrial society replete with all the distractions of technology (traffic, pagers, video games, busy schedules, e-mail, schoolwork, jobs, cell phones, iPods, and all the rushing about we all do in general), as well as the illnesses that still haunt Native people and are often the result of difficult living conditions, all require, more than ever, the arts of medicine people.

Storyteller by Roxanne Swentzell
(Santa Clara Pueblo), 2000.

CHAPTER TWO

Word Magic

Stomp Dance

Sing it now.
Ai ai ai
ai ai ai
This dance
this song
ai ai ai
will continue,
ai ai ai
will continue.
We know the sound
that calls us to sing
silent songs
that we sing
in our hearts.
Not with words
that can be traced
to vacant lands,
eyes and soundless hearts.
Voices
greet the night,
cedars bright

in a world laced
with silence.
Ai ai ai
ai ai ai
ai ai ai
Behind closed eyes
words remain.
Power is there
in a song,
in a breath,
in the place
of our dreams.
They tell us to be
afraid of the sounds
at night,
of turtle shells
singing in the distance.
How can we be afraid
of that which calls us home?
Ai ai ai

ai ai ai
Sing it again.
Ai ai ai
Turtle shells calling
us home.
Ai ai ai
This dance
Ai ai ai
Say it again
will continue.

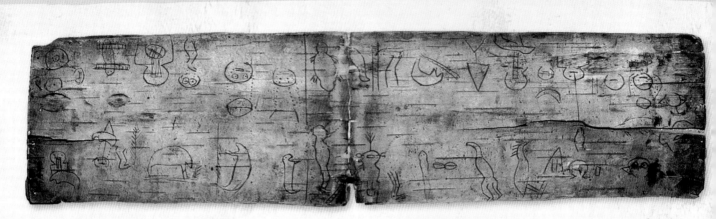

Ojibwe birchbark with song lyrics. Words recorded in this way suggest the importance of symbols and words in Native life.

Words are powerful things. Living things. They call up images, ideas, and feelings. They soothe. They hurt. Think of how we use language to console, or to tell about important events, or explain ideas. What if words could come to life? What if by saying something, it happened? Have you ever said something that hurt someone's feelings and then tried to "take it back"? In Native American beliefs, words and imagination are sacred, living things and must be treated with care and respect. Words are ceremony, connecting us to the living world. The ceremony reminds us of our connections to living things, to our ancestors who passed before us, and how the things they taught us through words are still living, because the words are still being spoken, still being sung. Songs are spoken words set dancing. When we sing, we are seeing words take shape, and those songs become living beings. Powerful magic can be set in motion by simply speaking the name of a spirit, or by singing about what you most desire. Once spoken, words can take on a life of their own, begin to breathe and take their place in the world, and so language must be used cautiously. An Inuit poem from the far North speaks of this:

Earliest Times

They say
in the early days
there were humans and animals living on the land and seas.
At this time, Animals could become Humans,
and Humans could become Animals, if this was their wish.
Often, there was no difference: People, Animals, all the same;

for their languages were one, at this time.
Words were powerful then. Magical, they say.
And human thoughts could have curious powers.
Stray words might make things turn out strangely;
they could begin to live on their own.
If a person wanted something to happen,
he had only to say it.
This is how it was, in the earliest times,
they say.

LIVING CHARMS

Even the breath that carries words is a sacred thing. Many tribes believe that breath is a kind of wind, granting life and health to people—or illness and death when it blows ill wishes. Speaking and sending out one's breath could be a kind of magic, a way of sending desires out into the world.

Breath, air, words, and wind in particular are thought to have great healing powers. A spoken charm describing the effect of the wind upon the land could restore health to the sick. The words of such a charm would help to bring good winds to the ill person and remove all bad winds from the body. Even the simplest charm could be, through its poetic language, a powerful thing of magic, allowing the human imagination to enter the beauty of the living land, as this Pima Wind-Medicine Song from Arizona shows:

> FAR ON the desert ridges
> The Cactus stands;
> Its blossoms swaying back and forth
> The blossoms swaying, swaying.

But language and word magic are not only for use by humans. Every living thing can make use of language. Even plants can speak of their desires and use words to help themselves. Everything has its own songs. In the deserts of the Southwest, the plants use their own language to help bring the much-needed rains.

"THEY ARE BEAUTIFUL! See the cloud,
        the cloud appears!"
"They are beautiful! See the rain, the rain comes near!"
Who spoke?
It was the little ear of corn
high on the stalk,
speaking while it looked at me:
"Ah, the floods are moving here, perhaps—
Ah, may the floods come this way!"
—*from a corn-grinding song, Zuni, New Mexico*

THE POWER OF NAMING

Many animals took their shapes through the use of words and names. Naming is a sacred business in all tribes. Names can give meaning to a person or event, or help establish relationships between people, animals, the land, and sacred powers. Great care always needs to be taken when speaking a name. Speaking or calling the name of an animal or spirit could call that being to the speaker. Or a name spoken at a certain time could change the shape of people or events. Sometimes speaking a name aloud can bring out the inner nature of a person or creature. In this way magic words, and even animal sounds and secret animal names, are like keys, unlocking the hidden talents and powers that people hold deep inside themselves.

LEFT: Cloud *kachina*, Hopi, 1850. Everything in the natural world has a name, a place, and is represented in man-made objects: The designs on the face represent clouds and rain. Objects such as this help start a conversation with the natural world.

OPPOSITE: A representation of a crow with a pearl eye, cut from a sheet of copper. Hopewell Mounds Culture, Ohio, 300 BCE–500 CE. Crows and ravens frequently appear in many Native stories as tricksters and shapeshifters.

AT THIS TIME, Crow-woman, Ka`ka, who was still walking on two legs, was hunting for clams. Then five trout boys came to visit her at her house. "Ka`ka!" the trout boys shouted. "Look! The other trout are destroying your home." Well, she didn't listen to them. They called and called again, "Ka`ka, the trout are destroying your home." After a long time, she came to look and see what was happening. She turned her head this way, and then the other way. "My name is not Ka`ka," she said at last. "My name is Kwolkwe`lbulo." At that moment she flew and became a crow.

—*Skagit, Puget Sound, Northwest Coast*

THE DANGER OF IDLE CONVERSATION

But people have to be careful. Even the most simple words or meaningless statements can become powerful, or even dangerous.

One time, among the Malecite people, near what is now New Brunswick, Canada, a monster was holding all the water, so that the rivers did not flow. Lakes dried up, and all the People were dying of thirst. Messengers were sent, but nothing could convince the monster to let the waters flow freely. Finally, the People really started complaining, saying things like "I'm dry as a turtle." Or "I'm thirsty as a fish." Or "I'm dry as a frog." At last a great man was sent to confront the monster. Even after hearing how thirsty everyone was, the monster still refused to release the waters. So this great man cut down a tree that fell upon the monster, killing it. The body of the tree became a huge river, and its branches became its streams and brooks. As the water began to flow again past the villages, the People jumped quickly into the water to drink. It was then that their words

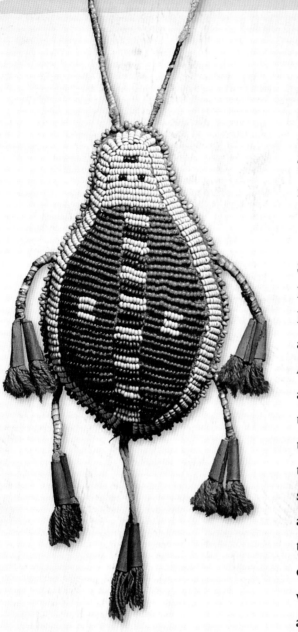

came to pass, and as they entered the water, they changed into the animals they had mentioned in their complaints: fishes, turtles, frogs, and more. Their words became true, and they were changed forever.

THE SEASON OF STORY

So words must be spoken carefully and correctly. Part of the power of words is related to when and how they are spoken. Certain stories and words are not appropriate for all times of the year. Among most tribes, stories of spirits and animals are not told except during the cold months, after the first snow. When the first spring rains come, those stories are put away again. It is believed that to speak of certain subjects during the summer months might anger the gods or the animal spirits and bring great misfortune upon the person and his family. For this reason, many of the most powerful stories are not told until winter, when many of the animals are gone or are hibernating.

Among the tribes of the Plains, winter has always been the time of telling stories. Imagine it. Winter is upon the land, animals are scarce, people are hungry. It is dark. The People are gathered in the lodge around a fire, and an old woman begins to speak. "Oh, this was long and long and long ago . . . ," she says. And as she speaks, her words take shape in the minds of the listeners and in the land. She speaks of the animals, living beneath the ground, held there by a greedy chief. The People were hungry. A boy was sent to trick the chief who held the animals. The boy was clever and fooled this chief. The animals were freed. Buffalo, deer, elk, birds, fish, all came up from below the ground. This is how it happened, she sings. In ancient times, she says, even now.

After she finishes telling the story, the men go outside the lodge. There are fresh tracks in the snow. The animals have come close. The hunt begins. The People will not starve.

THE POETRY OF MAGIC

This is just how word magic works: A story is told that takes the listeners back to the time when similar problems were solved or people were cured. Or a simple charm is made of words. Word magic reminds us of our connection to our ancestors, to the land upon which we live, of our traditions and our songs. The songs we sing and still hear are the same songs sung by our ancestors. The poem at the beginning of this chapter tells the story of the continuing tradition of the Stomp Dance, a ceremony practiced by the Cherokee, Choctaw, Seminole, Muskogee, and Chickasaw tribes of the Southeast. Even as the song is sung, generation to generation, it continues to live among the traditions of the People singing it. Beautiful, evocative language becomes a spell: calling the rain, healing the sick, changing the shapes of things. In this way, the events of the past are always happening and are always related to current events. The past is not dead, it's not even past; the stories told in the long ago are still weaving their way down into the present, still imparting wisdom to people who will listen. As long as the ancient stories are told, past and present are brought together for the good of the tribe. The stories of a people are their memory. A myth is a vessel, a container, holding the dreams, fears, joys, and hopes of a people. Beautiful language and powerful poetry keep traditions alive and strong in the world.

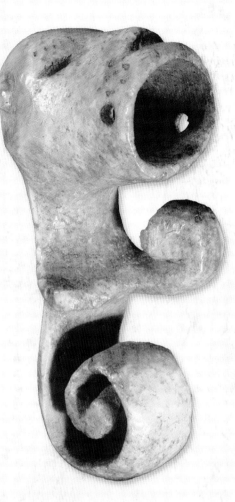

ABOVE: Spindle whorls were used by the Coast Salish during spinning to prevent the wool slipping from the spindle. The open mouth may represent the spirit's breath, song, or story. Objects such as this are the work of individual artists and their meanings often remain a mystery.

OPPOSITE: Beaded buckskin pouch in the form of a beetle, Crow, Plains.

Creation Legend by Tom Dorsey (Onondaga), 1946.

sinew,
bone and blood.
We are things of
spirit,
of earth,
of starlight,
of a spider's web
caught in the
brightness
of the sun.
Life was formed

Eight legs,
the ability
to float
from her body.
Grandmother Spider,
Creator of the world,
spun all of this
from a single
spinaret,
a single dream,
a prayer upon the waking

earth,
brought forth all
from the dream
of a silk
thread
and the daytime
star.

PART ONE

Telling the Land, Singing the Sky

Among many tribes, acts of creation are carried out by animals or by people with animal characteristics. Each culture had its own animal creators; sometimes the job was shared by a pair of animals whose actions and relationships were the basis of many stories. Among the Achumawi of Shasta County, California, Silver Fox and Coyote are the central characters in that tribe's creation story.

"OF COURSE, EVERYTHING HAS A BEGINNING . . ."

Many myths and legends begin with such a phrase, and of course, it is true. Everything known to people had to have an origin. Telling stories about those origins is an extremely important part of creation itself. Stories carry traditions. They instruct, inform, and record knowledge that allows the tribes to survive and maintain their cultural identities. Or, more simply, stories tell people who they are and where they come from, helping them take their place in the storied land.

Among Native Americans, stories have other uses as well. As we've already seen, special stories are used for healing. By telling or singing the story of the tribe's origin, the power of that seemingly distant time could be summoned into the present. That power could then be used by medicine men and women to heal the sick or bless the People. By bringing patients into the presence of "sacred time," they might be restored to health again. For this reason, it remains very important that the stories of creation are remembered and told.

OPPOSITE: Objects such as these Inuit combs are used in everyday activities such as grooming, but even everyday things may have otherworldly associations and figure in creation myths.

Silver Fox and Coyote Think of the World
(Achumawi)

Water was there.

The broad sky was clear. No clouds, no nothing. But after some time, a cloud formed, pulled together, and turned into Coyote. Below the cloud, fog appeared. This fog pulled together too, and this became Silver Fox. In this way, they became persons.

Well, Silver Fox and Coyote looked down from the sky and saw the world all filled with water. They sat and thought for a while. They thought about how nice a canoe would be and—there!—one appeared on the water.

They decided maybe this would be a good place. They said to each other, "Yes, let's stay here, this will be our home."

For a long time they floated around in that canoe. For a long time, they were on the water. The canoe started to smell. Coyote and Silver Fox got tired of this.

One day, Silver Fox told Coyote to lie down and rest. As Coyote lay sleeping, Silver Fox combed his coat and saved all the hair. Silver Fox kept combing until he had many hairs from the combings, and then he rolled, stretched, and flattened them in his hands.

He took these combings and spread them out over the water until they covered everything. This is how the earth was made by Silver Fox. He looked around and thought of many things: plants, trees, rocks, hills. They appeared just as he thought of them. Silver Fox thought of them and there they were.

Silver Fox barked to Coyote to wake up. Coyote jumped up and saw the rocks and trees and hills and wondered, "Where are we?"

"Hm, well, I don't know, really," Silver Fox replied. "We, um, just floated to shore somehow and here we are." Silver Fox didn't tell Coyote the truth; he didn't want Coyote to know that the world was his creation.

"Well, here is solid earth," said Silver Fox. "This looks like a good place. I'm going to live here." And with that, Silver Fox jumped out of the canoe. He was pretty happy to do this because, remember, that canoe wasn't smelling too nice.

Coyote got out too and they built a shelter. After a time, they thought about other things. They thought about people. Coyote and Silver Fox took small branches of serviceberry and pushed them into the ceiling of their house. After a certain time, these all turned into people with the names of animals, birds, and fishes. This is how it all came about. ☀

In this story, we are introduced to an amazing but sometimes confusing aspect of Native American myth: Often, animals are people and people are animals. In the early stages of creation, the People were the different kinds of animals. Forms changed. Often, there was no difference between the two.

Thought also plays an important role in this story. The world is filled by thinking of things that then appear. This ability did not belong only to deities and animals. Indeed, this power is still within the minds of men and women, and for this reason, people must always be careful what they think about. When our imaginations are sent out into the landscape, magical things can happen. Just as we must be careful with our words, we must be careful with our thoughts as well.

Imagination and thought are important elements in the myths of many Native American cultures. In the creation myth of the Pima of Arizona, unlike the previous story, a man (in man's form) is the creature that begins creation.

Song of the World
(Pima)

At this time, there was only darkness. Everywhere. Darkness and water. But there was movement and the darkness gathered together in some places and became thick, and after a certain time a man emerged from where the darkness was crowded together. Well, this man began walking around and thinking things over. He began to know himself and know that he was a man. There was a purpose in all of this.

From his body, from the place over his heart, he drew out a long stick, and this he used to feel his way through the darkness. Then from his body, he drew forth ants and placed them on the stick. The stick was made of greasewood, and the ants used resin from the stick to make a round ball. The man took this ball and placed it under his foot. He rolled his foot back and forth, back and forth over this ball, and this is the song he sang,

> *I make the world, and see!*
> *The world is finished.*
> *Now I make the world, and see!*
> *The world is finished.*

Well, he went on singing for some time and called himself the Maker of the World, and this was so. He sang slower, and the ball grew larger until, at the end of his song, the world was finished; there it was. He began to sing more quickly,

> *Let it go, let it go,*
> *Let it go, start it going!*

He took rocks, then, and made the stars and the constellations. He made the moon. All these things came from his body. The sun he made by making two large bowls, filling one with water and covering it with the other. Then he sat and thought about what he wanted, something brighter than the moon and stars. And because he thought this thing, it began to happen. The water turned into the sun and shone through the cracks in the bowls. He picked up the sun and placed it in the sky, and it is still there, just as he made it.

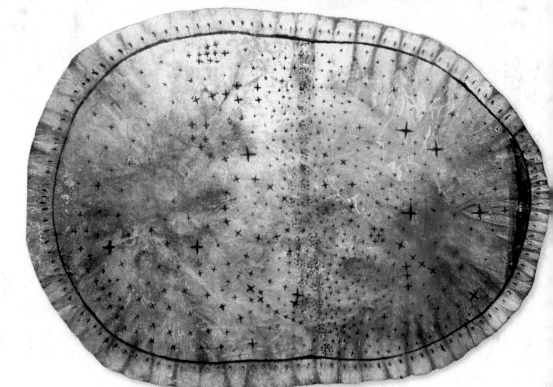

Pawnee buckskin star map, representing stars and constellations. As in the Akimel O'odham, or Pima, story, tales and images of stars and constellations also appear frequently in things that people make.

DIVING FOR EARTH

While important mythical events often occur in a special sequence or order, there isn't always a clear plan to the making of the world during the time of creation. Sometimes, events happen accidentally and the gods, like people, must make do the best they can.

The Flatterer Brings Up the Earth
(Cree)

Weesack-kachak, The Flatterer, grandson of the North Wind, was given a great responsibility.

The Creator had made all the animals and all the People and had put Weesack-kachak in charge of everything. Weesack-kachak was supposed to keep the animals and people from fighting and show everyone which plants and roots were good to eat, which for medicine, which for food. But Weesack-kachak did not follow the instructions of the Creator, and soon everyone was fighting. Oh, this was a bad time. Blood was everywhere on the ground, and the Creator was furious.

The Creator warned Weesack-kachak then. The Creator told him that if the bloodshed and the fighting did not stop, He would wash the stains from the ground in a way that nobody would like.

Well, Weesack-kachak did not believe the Creator's words. He made the animals and people fight. He played tricks on everyone. Finally, one day, the Creator had had enough. This is when the rains started. The rains began and did not end. Rivers overflowed their banks and the lakes grew higher and higher. Water was everywhere on the land. The sea rose so high that it also washed over all the land. Everyone was drowned except for one otter, one beaver, and one muskrat.

Weesack-kachak knew that this was his fault. He tried to stop the sea, but the waters were too strong for him. Then he cried and cried, right there, beside Otter, Beaver, and Muskrat.

Well, after a certain time, the rain finally stopped. Weesack-kachak and the three animals were there, floating on the flood. Weesack-kachak knew that he dare not ask the Creator for anything, so he sat, and thought and thought. His powers were limited. He could not create anything, but he could enlarge anything that was already there. This was his plan: Weesack-kachak thought that if he could get a piece of the old earth from the bottom of the sea, he might be able to make a little island for himself and the three animals to live on. But Weesack-kachak could not dive very deep and he thought that the earth he needed might be very far down. Now what was he going to do? Sadness washed over him again.

But the Creator was listening to Weesack-kachak's thoughts and told him that if he could get some of the old earth beneath the waters, he would give Weesack-kachak the power to remake everything else that had been lost.

So Weesack-kachak turned first to Otter and told him that if he could dive down to the bottom and get some earth, an island might be made from it and they would all be saved.

Otter tried three times, but came back with nothing.

Next, he asked Beaver. He hoped that Beaver could swim to the bottom.

Beaver dived three times as well. He dived very deep, but did not bring back any earth. Now Muskrat was their only hope.

Weesack-kachak praised Muskrat and promised him roots to eat and rushes for a house. He told Muskrat to dive straight and go quickly to the bottom.

So Muskrat dived, but came back with nothing. He dived again, but still was unable to bring back any earth. But this time Weesack-kachak smelled earth on his paws. Weesack-kachak told Muskrat to dive again, for only a tiny piece of earth was needed. Weesack-kachak promised Muskrat a fine wife who would bear him many children. It was a good deal. For a wife, Muskrat tried again.

Muskrat was down a long time—so long that they feared he was dead. But then there were some tiny bubbles. So Weesack-kachak reached way down and pulled Muskrat up, out of the water. Poor Muskrat was almost dead, but there, clutched tightly in his paw, was a small piece of earth.

Weesack-kachak took this and made land. Now, some say that he also got a piece of wood and a piece of bone and from them made trees and more animals. But some say this is not so. The Creator made those things again and took back his power from Weesack-kachak so all he could do was flatter and play tricks. Some say it happened like this.

DIFFERENT WAYS OF SEEING THE WORLD

The way a tribe survives, what the People live on (or their *subsistence*), and the rituals related to food are important parts of a tribe's myths and stories. Hunter-gatherer tribes (people who once relied mostly on food they hunted or found) tell stories of Earth Divers and of the magical creation of the land after a time when the world was covered in water. Such stories emphasize the important connections between human and animal relationships and interdependence. Agricultural societies (tribes that once obtained or still obtain most of their food from planting, raising, and harvesting crops) tell stories of emergence: myths of people growing out of the ground and emerging into the world as plants do.

LEFT: In the Southwest, stories or portions of stories, maps, clan signs, and cosmological symbols are recorded on the rocks and hills of the surrounding landscape.

OPPOSITE: Figurine of clay. Fremont culture, Utah, 1000 CE.

The Zuni of New Mexico know that before their emergence into this world, the People were much like lizards, with tails and webbed hands. The Hopi and other Pueblo tribes have stories that tell of ancestors who moved upward from the Lower World, finally entering the world we know, where they live to this day. Ancient rock art of the Southwest tells of these origins. The tribes of the Southeast believe that the ancestors emerged from the mounds and merged with the People of the sky, creating a new people. Oral traditions, stories, songs, and poems continue to teach of these origins today.

In the Southwest especially, "emergence" myths are the most common. These stories tell of a progression of worlds, establishing hierarchies (ranks and order of things) of animals, plants, events, and proper actions.

THE MIRROR OF MYTH

Myths are mirrors: They reflect the People who tell them and the People who lived before them. The present, the ancient past, and even reflections of other traditions or cultures may be caught and seen moving beneath the myth's surface. Even non-Indian people occasionally have a place in Native American stories . . .

Origin of the Adlet and Qadlunait
(Central Inuit)

A daughter lived alone with her old father and refused to marry. She had many suitors but turned each one down in his turn. This went on until, at last, a spotted white-and-red dog won her heart and she agreed to marry him. Eventually, they had ten children, five of whom were dogs, the other five Adlet. And even the Adlet were part dog. Everything below their waists was hairy all over (except the soles of their feet). All the children shared a tremendous appetite. They lived for nothing but food. Their father did not hunt at all, so the girl's father had to get the food for all of them, and this was a great deal of work. Soon the old man grew tired of having to hunt for his daughter's lazy husband and all their children, so this is what he did: He put the whole family in his kayak and left them on a small island to live. Every day, his wife's husband would swim across the inlet and get meat from the old man. When he did this, he hung his boots around his neck.

One day, the old man filled the boots with heavy rocks instead of meat, and when the dog tried to swim back to the island, the weight of the stones carried him straight to the bottom and he drowned. When the dog's boots washed up on the shore, the old man's daughter knew her husband was dead.

Right away, the daughter wanted to avenge her husband's death. She called all of her children together and sent them running to her father's home, where they fell upon the old man and ate his hands and feet. But the daughter was afraid that her father would come after her children and try to kill them. So the five Adlet she sent away inland to hunt animals, and they became the ancestors of many Indian peoples. From her husband's boots, she made a boat and sent the five puppies far across the sea and sang to them, "My children, when you are there, across the sea, many wondrous things you will make, from these things, much joy will come to you." So the dog children floated far over the ocean and arrived in the land beyond the sea and became the ancestors of the Europeans. ☀

So you see, everything in Native American stories, even people living far away from North America, had a beginning.

PART TWO

The First Wonderful Things

Everything has an origin, even things used or seen every day all have an important part in the beginning of things and Native life as a whole. Stories about the origins of objects (like fire) or skills (like weaving) often contain important information about how those things were to be thought about and interpreted and used for the benefit of the People.

These stories also tell the People which deities, spirits, and/or animals are connected with certain objects or elements in nature, and tell how they should be honored. These myths also show how important thought and imagination are in any acts of creation.

MAKING FIRE AND LIGHT

Even after the creation of essential things like earth and people, the process was far from finished. Indeed, people (animal and human) were to play important roles in the ever-developing drama of this creative process. People were there, animals too, but what about all the *things*? Fire? Light? Trees? How did all the other things come about? Two stories—the first from the Southeast, the second from California—speak of these matters.

Inuit soul boat. In kayaks, Northern peoples traveled far, even from one world to another, finding and creating stories wherever they went.

Bears Lose Fire to Man
(Alabama)

Oh, bears were always greedy. They never wanted to part with anything. This was the time when bears owned fire, but because they were always hungry, the bears left the fire alone and went to look for berries. Fire waited and waited. It was hungry too. Soon, Fire had enough of all this waiting around and started to cry out, "Please, I am hungry, someone feed me or I will die." Some human people heard the noise and followed it until they came to the fire. It had almost died. Those people got sticks of wood from the north, south, east, and west and laid them on the fire. Well, this was much better and the fire began to grow again until it was a good-size blaze. After a certain time, the bears returned from eating to get their fire. Fire spat at them and said, "Bears, bah! I don't know you anymore." So the bears left without the fire, and humans had it from then on.

How Light Began
(Gallinomero)

It was so dark. All the animals were running about, bumping into one another. In the dark skies, birds flew, but they, too, were always flying into one another and falling out of the sky. There was no light at this time. Coyote and Hawk thought about the problem. They thought a long time about the darkness and finally came to a decision.

TOP: Pipe in the form of a seated woman, Lakota, South Dakota. Basic elements, such as fire and light, have important places in myth, and consequently objects associated with them are often highly decorative.

BOTTOM: An unusual storage bag made from seagulls' feet and bleached sealskin, decorated with an appliqué design made from unbleached sealskin, Inuit, Greenland. The design symbolizes the sun, or more generally, light. The bag was employed to store the moss used to make the wicks for seal-oil lamps. Not surprisingly, Northern cultures, living in the longest nights, have strong artistic traditions of creating light-making and light-holding artifacts.

Coyote moved slowly in the darkness and felt around until he came to a swamp. Still feeling around, he collected some dry reeds. Twisting them, turning them, twisting them again, he made a ball of the dry reeds. On his way back, he found some flints on the ground. Coyote gave the flints and the reed ball to Hawk. Right away, Hawk knew what to do with them. Hawk flew high up into the sky and used the flints and made the ball burn, and this burning ball he sent spinning, spinning, spinning around the world. Down below, something was still bothering Coyote. It was still very dark at night. Another ball was made, but this time, the reeds were damp, and so when Hawk lit them on fire with the flints, they did not burn so well. The moon is not as bright as the sun. Now you know why this is so.

A finger mask, representing the moon spirit, used by women during social dances, Yupik, Alaska. Like the Gallinomero and Alabama stories, many tribal groups associate the bringing of light to the earth as a cooperative act between humans and animal spirits.

DAY AND NIGHT

Many of the first things were obtained from animal people or given by them—gifts from our cousins. The process of creating things is often accomplished by careful thought, negotiation, deliberation and—because animals, like people, are not perfect—fighting and arguing. In this way, the division of day and night was determined by animals. A story from the Iroquois of the Northeast tells how this happened.

Porcupine Determines Day and Night

All the animals were fighting. This was a long time ago and Porcupine was the leader of all the animals. Porcupine had asked them, "Do you think night is best, darkness all the

RIGHT: A spindle whorl. Inuit, Coast Salish, late nineteenth/early twentieth century. Used in weaving to prevent the wool from slipping from the spindle. In many native cultures, weaving, whether a basket or a rug, is seen as as an act of creation with strong mythic meaning.

BELOW: Seal oil lamp, Inuit. A lamp such as this would have helped bring light to the dark winter nights of the Northern world.

time, or should we have daylight all the time?" This is why the animals were fighting. They could not decide.

Some wanted daylight all the time; others wished for darkness. Now Chipmunk wanted to have night and day alternate—he wanted seasons, months, weeks. He began to sing, "Day will come, day will come, light, light, light will come." Chipmunk repeated his song.

But Bear disagreed, so he began to sing, "Darkness, darkness, night is best; this is how it will be."

Chipmunk's song was pretty good, he sang well, so these things started to happen. The song was very strong, and as he sang, dawn began to appear over the mountains. This made the other animals furious, and Bear began to chase Chipmunk. Now, Chipmunk is very fast and he got away, but not before Bear's claws left their mark on his back. But this was a small price to pay. Night and day have taken turns ever since.

WORDS AND SKILLS

Words are an important aspect of setting things in their proper order (as seen in the next chapter). In the previous story, songs are required to make the day and night change back and forth. Cleverness and the power of song changed the world forever. Among many tribes, battles or contests between magicians and medicine people are likewise fought or carried out at the level of language. Battles of words and songs decided many important events and established both the personal power of the singer and the magical possibilities of language.

In ancient and mythic times, many skills were learned from animal people or the gods. These skills were considered sacred and magical, and their practice often required certain kinds of rules to ensure that the ability would not be lost. These skills have been handed down through oral tradition over countless generations, often hearkening back to an ancient time when they were bestowed by animals or holy beings.

Weaving is still an important skill among many tribes (including those of the Northwest coast, as well as the Hopi and Navajo), and its history is deeply connected to the myths and traditions of Native North America. In the Southwest, weaving became a highly developed art, and some tribes, like the Navajo, are still known for their exquisitely woven rugs and textiles.

The First Weaving
(Navajo)

The People were told that there was a place in the Lower World where two rivers crossed. The place was called "Fine-fiber Cotton." Two people there carried up the seed of that plant; they were spider people. They said that people should use the plant for clothing instead of wearing the skins of animals. So it happened that this seed was planted in the earth.

After a time the plant ripened, and the cotton was gathered, and the People fashioned a small wheel, no more than four inches round, and they put a slender stick through the middle of it. This was used in the spinning of cotton. Then the chief medicine woman said, "You must always spin toward yourself, for then beautiful things come to you; do

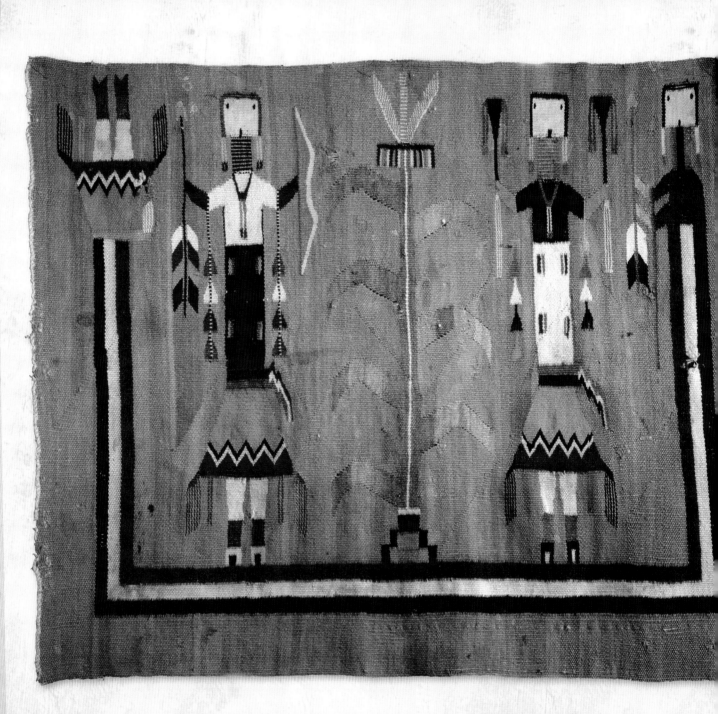

ABOVE: Navajo blanket based on a sandpainting design. Two supernatural "holy people" flank the sacred maize (corn) plant, which was their gift to the People. They are enclosed by a rainbow arc, representing the connection between the People, the land, and rain.

OPPOSITE: Fiber apron worn by female basketmakers, Anasazi, early seventh century. The Anasazi were an early Southwestern culture, from which many contemporary Southwestern tribes claim descent.

not spin away from you." The People wished to make cloth with which to trade for shell and turquoise beads. She knew their thoughts. Again she said, "You must spin toward you, or the beautiful things will fly from you."

Spider Man devised names for every part of the spinning process and all the tools used to spin. Spider Woman changed all of the names. Finally Spider Man said, "Before you now you see everything that we have named for you. It is yours to work with and to use, following your own wishes. But from now on when a baby girl is born to your tribe, you shall go and find a spider web that is woven at the mouth of a hole; you must take it and rub it on the baby's hand and arm. Do this and when she grows up, she will weave and her fingers and arms will never tire from the weaving."

The weaving progressed, and they made all kinds of useful articles. There were many kinds of weaving. Thread was made, feather blankets, fur blankets, mats for the floors of their homes and for hanging in front of the entrances. The People lived peacefully and were happy in discovering designs with their new art. They raised great quantities of corn. All this made them grow in number; they became a very strong people.

ALL PART OF THE TELLING

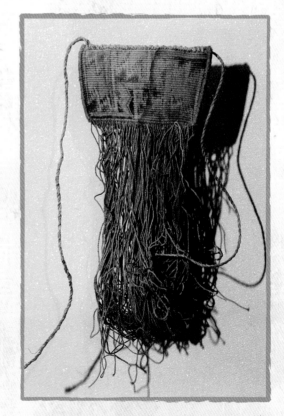

Think of the stories you know or have been told throughout your life. Perhaps stories that at first seemed only entertaining became more meaningful as you thought more about them. Perhaps you have been told stories of your own family, your ancestors, the lands upon which they lived, or the place where you live now. We all have stories within us; some are told to us, others we find.

As long as the stories are told, creation is never entirely completed. It is an ever-cycling event. People have important roles to play in this regard, and because the process is always continuing, people must be ever aware, ever knowledgeable about the past, while looking forward to the future with hope, caution, and delight.

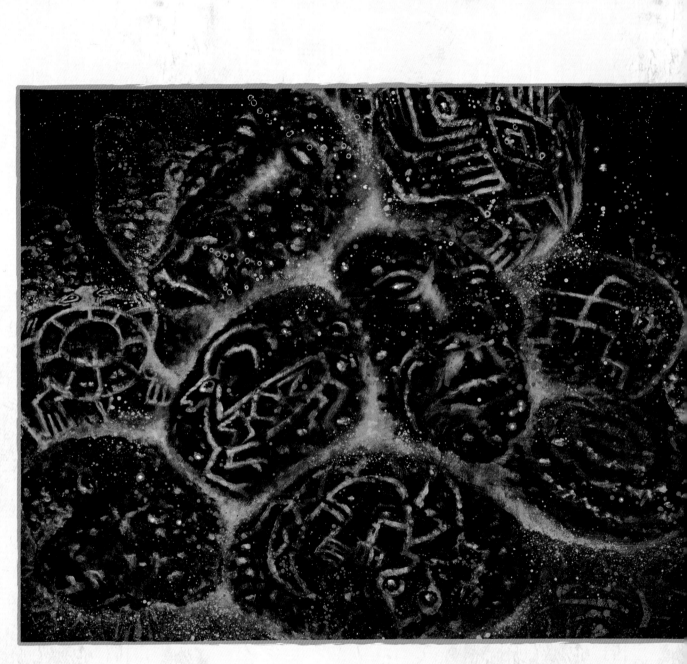

Stone People of the Sweatlodge by S. D. Nelson (Standing Rock Sioux/Lakota), 1995.

CHAPTER FOUR

Charming a Stone
The Magic of Art & Artifacts

Coyotesse

Here,
she said,
snapping back hair
so red,
I give you these things.
A small bone,
white,
like the sun,
a turtle shell,
to remind you of water,
the place from which
you came.
When you stand
upon the earth,
you will remember my name,
shooting stars
under a dark,
pinpoint lit
starlight sky,
you will remember me,
Ohoyo, estonko,
I'll whisper turtle shells
and you will know
you are
my daughter.

ABOVE: Lakota bead and buckskin doll. Such objects were made with painstaking care and attention to detail by grandmothers for their grandchildren, imbuing a special "magic" in these objects. This doll reproduces a woman's riding equipment and adult costume with great precision.

OPPOSITE, LEFT: Kethawn, Navajo, early twentieth century. A stone such as this one would be left as an offering at shrines, as well as carried for protection while traveling.

OPPOSITE, RIGHT: Hopi representation of Shalako Mana, the female companion of the Shalako *kachina*. As the giver of life, the sun is personified as both male and female and celebrated in many forms throughout Native America.

Nearly everyone has special objects in his or her possession. A lucky charm. A stone picked up on a journey and kept. A doll given by a family member as a special gift. Perhaps something that belonged to a departed family member or ancestor. Objects, artifacts, and art can become deeply related to our family's memories of the past. Art can change the way we see the world. Certain objects or artifacts can remind us of places we've been and adventures we've had or, like a jar made from clay, are built from things found near the places where we have lived. There is magic and power in remembering the stories of the gifts we've found or been given.

There have always been special, or sacred, objects known to Native American people. Some of these might be personal objects, such as carvings carried for good luck or for protection. Other artifacts might be kept by a specific family for generations. The most sacred objects, often kept in special bags, wrappings, or containers called medicine bundles, are for the use of the entire tribe. These bundles can hold feathers, stones, carvings, or other important items. Such objects are closely related to the history of the tribe, and ceremonies are held when the bundles are opened or shown in public. Often these sacred objects are things that have been found and kept for long periods of time.

When magical objects are created, there are many questions raised as the artist sits down to work his or her magic. What am I going to make? What does the material say about itself? (Does the stone look like an

animal, a face, or an arrowhead?) What will be the use of this creation; what is its purpose? Sometimes material is chosen because it has special qualities of shape or association. Maybe the stone comes from a sacred place on the land. Or perhaps the antler used in a charm comes from an animal killed during an important hunt. Or the root of a certain tree, like the cottonwood, is used for a carving of a rain spirit because that tree's root has the ability to find water, even in the desert.

People are not alone in making art. Even the smallest animals can create things of beauty. Even the smallest animals have power and can help set things right in the world. Beautiful things are being made all the time and can still work great wonders. A tiny web of silk, a small jar of earth, can hold a glowing ember of the sun to help light the world.

Grandmother Spider Steals the Sun
(Cherokee)

In the darkness, the People were frightened.
They turned to the animals for comfort.
The animals had sight, for in their world there was sight in darkness.
Fox, having pity on the People, said,
"There are places in the world where there is light,
but the ones who have it are too greedy to share.
Our people are frightened, they cannot see.

RIGHT: Early spider gorget, Mississippian. The crossed logs on the thorax symbolize Grandmother Spider's sacrifice to bring the Sacred Fire to the Mississippian people.

OPPOSITE: A jar made from the earth with scalloped collar and incised design. Haudenosaunee, 1500 CE.

Who will bring light to our people?"

Possum stood tall. "My tail is large, and I can carry the light there."

The animals agreed.

So Possum, being very brave and strong,

journeyed to the sun's house.

It was beautiful, so light, and full of life.

Possum snatched a piece of light from the sun and hid it in his tail.

Soon a strange warmth spread through his bottom,

burning hotter and hotter.

Smoke began to rise, and Possum knew he was on fire!

The sun had burnt his hairs right off!

He stopped to rest at the river's edge to put the fire out.

The greedy people who had the sun

found Possum holding his bare tail,

and took the piece of the sun from him.

(To this day, Possum's tail has no hair!)

Buzzard next stood tall and strong.

"My wings are strong and I can fly to the sun's house,

take a piece, and put it on my head to light my way home."

So Buzzard flew and flew and flew and flew

until he reached the house of the sun.

It was so beautiful, and there was light all around.

Buzzard flew to the sun and took a piece when she wasn't looking.

He placed it upon his head to light his way.

Soon, he began to feel a warmth upon his head. That warmth quickly got hotter.

He began to sweat and sweat, the burning was so great.

He swooped low to the ground to rest, and the greedy people saw him.

They snatched the fire from his head and took it back
    to the sun's house.

(To this day, Buzzard's head is bald and red from
    where the sun burned her red mark!)

Now, of all the animals who loved the People

and wanted to help them,

there was Grandmother Spider, weaver of stories and songs,

the smallest of the animals who loved the People.

She stood tall to the other animals. "Let me try."

The other animals loved and respected Grandmother Spider.

In spite of her tiny size

and frail body, she could weave words and music,

and her weavings were the strength that had held the animals

and the People together.

First, Grandmother Spider made a jar from the earth, drying it with her breath.

Under the cover of darkness, she next wove a web from one side of the earth to the other.

Grandmother Spider was so tiny and frail that those greedy people paid her no mind!

When she reached the house of the sun, Grandmother Spider reached far and
    snatched a piece of the sun, placing it in her jar made from the earth.

She ran with her tiny legs upon her web that brought her home.
She took from her pot the piece of the sun,
and it was so warm, and beautiful,
like the house of the sun.
Grandmother Spider,
tiny and frail,
brought the sun to the People,
in a jar of clay,
so there would be darkness
no more.

A COLLECTION OF WONDERFUL THINGS

The Blackfeet people have been keepers of the Beaver Bundle since the beginning. It is a holy thing, and we should not say too much about it. Inside are the skins of animals, stones, and objects—one for every story and song known by the keeper of the bundle. Hundreds of things. Hundreds of songs. Each one passed down since the earliest times. We will never see the Beaver Bundle, for it is only taken out at certain ceremonies and then only in the presence of people who have earned the right to be there when it is opened.

We will never see the Beaver Bundle, but when we go into places where ancient things are kept, we can imagine that each one of those carvings, weavings, and paintings is trying to tell us a story. Those objects may no longer be held by the People who made them, but they still have stories to tell. Sometimes the tales are broken, like pieces of pottery bespeaking a whole that we cannot completely put back together, but even small things tell a story, or beg us to imagine one.

Imagine standing in a room in a large museum. As you look around the dimly lit gallery, you begin to recognize shapes: a basket, an arrow, a beautifully decorated carving, a shield. Some of the objects are unrecognizable to you. What if these objects could speak? What would they tell you about themselves? How have they been used? Where did they come from? How did they get to this museum? Whom do they belong to? Here are some of things that you may see . . .

Blackfoot *iniskim*, or buffalo stones.

Curious Brown Stones Wrapped in Buffalo Hide

Sometimes stones look like buffalo, even though they have not been carved. Because of this resemblance, the stones are kept by the Blackfeet people. In times of poor hunting, when the People are starving and the animals will not come, the iniskim, or "buffalo stone" is taken out. Special songs are sung by its keeper, the story of the stone's finding is told, and then stone itself begins to sing, *The buffalo will all come back, the buffalo will all come back. The buffalo will come back to the People. A hungry woman found me long ago and brought me to her people. Remember me. Sing my song.* The People keep these stones for times of need, and when another is found upon the land, it is considered a great blessing.

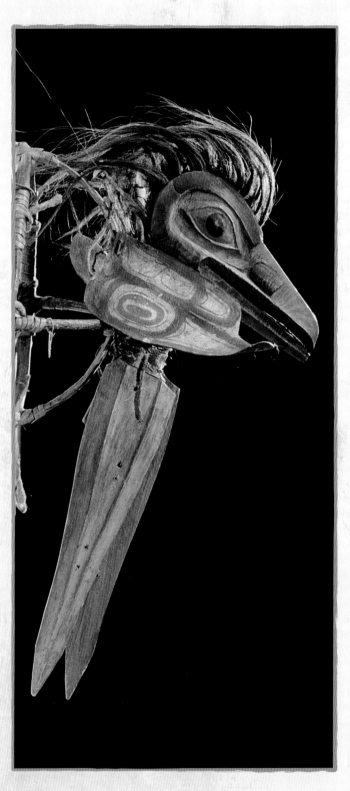

Raven headdress from the Northwest coast.

A Headdress, Brightly Painted

Made of cedarwood, a Raven headdress from the Northwest coast has human hair set into it. Its large eyes can see many things. By wearing this headdress, the wearer could become Raven, could speak as Raven speaks, could see as Raven sees, could dance as Raven dances. "I stole the sun," Raven says. "Me! I! I stole the sun and put it in the sky for all the People! Say thank you!" Raven cries. But now the mouth is quiet, for the headdress has not been worn for a long time. Perhaps objects such as this are living things, and happiest when they are dancing.

A Simple Red-Ware Pot

Lots of pottery was used by the People of the deserts in southern Arizona, the Tohono O'odham. Wine was made from the fermented fruit of the tall saguaro cactus. Women gathered the fruit with long sticks that knocked the fruit from the cactus's top onto the ground. The wine is kept in vessels and used for ceremonies and other special occasions. The men drink the wine to call the clouds. They drink and drink and sing and sing. Their songs become clouds thrown up to the sky. The rains will come—tomorrow, or the day after, they will come.

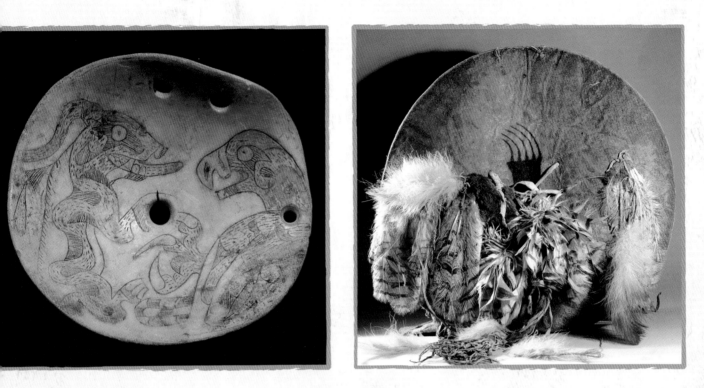

LEFT: Stylized shell gorget, Mississippian. RIGHT: Crow shield made from tough shrunken buffalo skin.

A Shell Pendant, or Gorget

The pendant, which would be worn around the neck, resting on the chest, shows a water panther, a mythical creature who lives in rivers and lakes in the Southeast, confronting a bird of prey. A warning? A call to war? Images such as this evoke powerful feelings in both the wearer and all who see it.

A War Shield Decorated with Feathers

A shield does not only protect the body. Painted with special symbols and designs, with feathers attached, the shield also provides magical protection, granting bravery and strength to the warrior. What happens when a shield is captured and kept? What happens to its power when it comes to be held by someone other than who first held it? There was once a song woven into it: *No arrow finds me, no arrow finds me, no arrow finds me. The way is clear before me. I come. The earth is mine.*

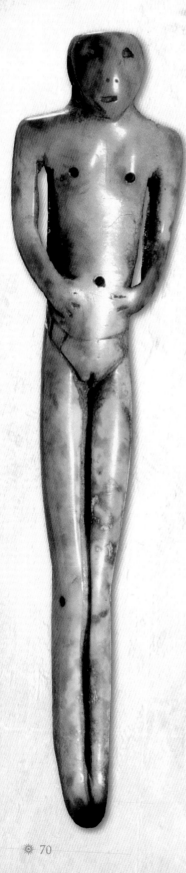

A Simple Needle Case, Carved of Bone

The most beautiful things begin with stitches: beadwork, decorative clothing, fringes on bags and breeches. Inside a small container carved in human form, needles are kept so they will not be lost. Perhaps inside there are eight or ten needles of different size, made of bone. What wonderful things have they stitched? Clothing sewn by hand with these needles kept someone warm and alive through a terrible winter. Perhaps, when summer came at last, a grandmother gave this needle case to her granddaughter and told her to keep her stitches tight and make beautiful things for her children.

A Hoop Strung with Sinew

All tribes played games. One of the most common was a game played with sticks and a hoop. Sometimes the hoop would be rolled along the ground, then people would chase after it, trying to throw their sticks through the hoop without knocking it over. In this way, young people also trained for the hunt. Older children, when they became more skilled at the game, might even try to shoot arrows through the hoop. But the hoop was not just a toy. Often the hoop was strung to depict a symbol of the sun, and in this way reminded people of the Sacred Twins, who also liked to play games. Many tribes have stories about Twins, about brothers who rise from obscure origins to become heroes, to become great protectors of their people. It is said that, one time, the Twins found their father's game equipment and set off on a journey to find him. Their grandmother told them not to go. Their father was the sun, you see, and the journey to his home is always long and challenging. But the Twins dropped the hoop upon the ground and off it went, all by itself. They followed it to the sun's house, and met their father. Many strange things happened to them along the way, but that is another story, and the hoop is already far from us, moving low on the horizon.

A Painted Figure, Carved from Cottonwood

Among the Pueblo people of the Southwest (the Hopi especially), dolls, called *kachinas*, or *kats'ina*, are given to children to teach them about all the spirits and ancestors in the Pueblo world. Some are monsters; some depict rain, clouds, and snow; some are connected to mountains or parts of the land; others are carved to represent powerful spirits whose stories are important parts of Pueblo oral tradition and must not be forgotten.

Arrowheads Made of Flint or Chert

Arrowheads can be found in every part of North America. Though they are no longer used for hunting, arrowheads still have traditional uses. They are considered lucky when found on open ground. Medicine people among the Navajo and other tribes use them for healing and for protection. It is believed that arrowheads still hold part of the power and purpose of their making. When you hold one in your hand, you wonder: Who made this thing? What was the name of its maker? How has it survived so long? Will it bring me luck and keep me safe upon my road?

TOP: Hopi runner *kachina*.

BOTTOM, LEFT AND RIGHT: Flint and chert arrowheads, Sandia Mountains, New Mexico.

OPPOSITE: Inuit needle case carved in the form of a female figure.

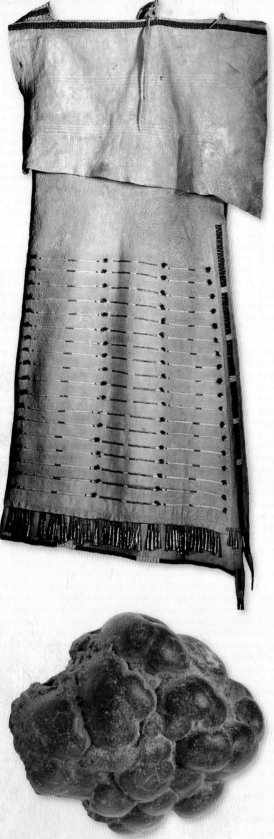

A Dress Adorned with Quillwork

In the days before the Europeans came, clothing on the Plains was decorated with quillwork: Tiny porcupine quills were dyed and worked onto clothing, bags, pipe-stems and other special items. How beautiful the quillwork is! Later, beads were often traded between Europeans and Native Americans, and even later, between the tribes themselves. The beads often replaced earlier quillwork. Colors rise from the surface of the dress to your eyes. Whose hands stitched this dress? Who wore the dress? Perhaps it was made for a special occasion. What did the old woman say, upon seeing her granddaughter's beautiful quillwork dress? Did it remind her of the night sky filled with bright stars? Or of the red hills rising from the Plains?

A Simple Stone

Much worn and polished by handling over the years, the stone could be almost anything. From one side, it looks like a buffalo, yet it has not been carved. Or perhaps it has another form that only you can see and imagine. What story does the simple stone tell? Where did it come from? Isn't it like stones you yourself have picked up on your travels? Why do we keep such things? Reminders of all that has gone before, perhaps they keep us.

TOP: 1830s Lakota buckskin and quillwork dress.

BOTTOM: A stone of antiquity, New Mexico.

Early white earthenware jar painted with spirals. Anasazi pottery is highly prized, widely collected, and frequently looted. Chaco Canyon, New Mexico.

LOST AND FOUND

We have seen wonderful things. But there are many questions left unanswered. How do such objects come to rest in museums? Where were they found? How were they gotten? Is it better for special objects to stay with the families and people who created them? It's a dilemma. Scholars learn a lot from ancient objects, and burials can tell us a great deal about what life was like in the past. But human remains are part of those burials and many times the descendants of the deceased still live on the lands where those burials took place or can remember where they are. And what about artifacts taken from the ground? Some of these objects were intentionally put into the ground with their owners at the time of death and were never meant to see the sun again. However, they were removed from their resting places by individuals taking what did not belong to them to sell and make a profit. Many artifacts that have ended up in non-Native hands were taken unlawfully from Native peoples.

The beauty and commercial value of these objects can make people greedy, even people who should know better. Once, at a western pueblo, a small ritual statue was stolen. That small statue was an important part of a ceremony known to only one woman. The statue was stolen from her by people she knew—young people of the village who had forgotten the stories and wanted only money. That statue was sold to collectors and ended up in a gallery in New York. Someone bought it and put it on a shelf in his or her home, in the living room. Learning that the statue was gone, the People of the village asked the old woman if another statue could be made and the ceremony continue as it always had. "No," she said, "there was only one, only one statue that came to me down through the years from those ancient times. Now I shall never sing those songs again; that story is over."

Yes, there is a great deal that such artifacts might teach us, but they also serve an important purpose by being left where they were intentionally kept, buried, or placed. Objects in the earth tell a special kind of story. People remember those things, and stories are told of them. Some objects are left at shrines and serve important ritual purposes. These are offerings to the spirits of the land they are left upon. Their exact locations may even be forgotten in time or may be well-guarded secrets, but memories of their existence and their placement in the earth or at shrines inform part of a people's "landscape memory" and their ability to live well upon that land. Sometimes artifacts are buried or hidden so that they may live on in the imaginations of the People who made them.

Today, ethical museums work with tribes and have returned many ancient things. Many beautiful creations have been returned to their people, returned to the earth from which they came. Today, tribes are performing important work with museums in interpreting the meaning of ancient creations, helping to tell the right stories of those wonderful and powerful objects made long ago. Museums and tribes are working together to heal the actions of the past and make sure that the artifacts in museums are treated properly.

These objects, and the powers they contain and represent, help build and maintain strong connections between Native people, landscape, ancestors, spirits, gods, and people from other cultures who are curious about the beauty of the Native American world. These creations continue to inspire questions and wonder, wherever they are found, seen, and remembered.

Anasazi pot shards can be widely found throughout the American Southwest. Fascinating reminders of that land's ancient past, they may be appreciated but should be left where they are found, as the Ancestors intended.

Gathering from Four Directions by Tony Abeyta (Navajo), 1999.

CHAPTER FIVE

Out Upon the Land
Hunters, Heroes, & Travelers

Hunting the Air for Water in the Desert

Nashoba,
the wolf, is hungry.
Hunting rabbits
is what she does.
Sniffing seashells, rose
    quartz,
limestone,
and the air
for a scent
of the hunt.
Traces of lace teacup
    remnants
or flowers,
scent stuck
to fragrant petals
fragile
in their resistance.

Nashoba,
the wolf,

is hunting.
For water,
for life
the scent of water
is everywhere in sharp
    needles
tufts of flowering
migration,
sagebrush
and bottle grass,
calling to her, she lifts her
snout,
scents the air
for drink,
hunting
water,
in her blood
she cannot deny the call
of ancestors,
she remembers

in her dreams.
She speaks to stones,
statues, rocks
and shards of glass.
Everything
tells a story.
Nashoba,
the wolf,
is hunting words on a
    prayer rising,
forming
like frost
breath to heaven
and the words
that live in her head like
    water,
she cannot
forget,
nor does she cease
the hunt.

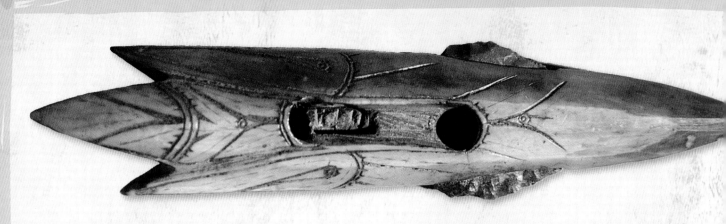

THE HUNT FOR FOOD

In our modern times, most of us buy the food we need. How many of us have actually hunted for our food? Even if we have been hunting or fishing, was the hunt important to our survival? Would we starve if the hunt went badly? It is hard to imagine how important a successful hunt would have been to Plains tribes in earlier times. While many tribal people now purchase most of their foodstuffs, some tribes (especially in the Arctic) still rely heavily upon hunted food. For tribes that depend on hunting, starvation is always a possibility should the hunt go badly. Because no hunt is ever a sure thing, special actions are necessary to help improve the odds . . .

ON THE GREAT PLAINS, a hunting party is preparing itself. Spears are sharpened. The horses are painted with powerful symbols: lightning designs, handprints, lines of color moving quickly across their shoulders and flanks. The horses will fly like lightning. They will bear down upon the prey, allowing their riders to strike. Their hooves are wind-born and will not be slowed by the weight of their rider.

TOP: Inuit harpoon head made from ivory with inset chert blades. Weapons used for hunting are imbued with power by engraving them with special designs and symbols.

BOTTOM: Charms used to aid hunting are sometimes made to include forms of animals to be hunted, or who were themselves great hunters. This Inuit hunting charm depicts a polar bear's head (a great hunter), two seal heads (the hunted), and a man's head, for man learned to hunt seals from Polar Bear and so stands between the two.

IN THE COLD NORTHERN LANDS, a band of Inuit take to the sea in their boats made from the skin of the bearded seal. Walrus have been seen. The sea is calm, but the men's hearts are racing. Charms have been tied to the boat and to their weapons to help them in the hunt. Carved from walrus ivory and seal bone, these figures represent the hunted animals; they are pieces of power that will guide the weapons to the animals' bodies.

A DANGEROUS BUSINESS

Unlike grocery shopping, hunting was a dangerous business! A hunt could take you many miles from your home, far out to sea, across many landscapes, through many adventures. Because of this, the hunter needed help upon his road. A special song, a powerful image painted upon his horse, a magical carving, knowledge of the land, and understanding of animal behaviors: all these things would be essential to a successful hunt.

Early Plains effigy of a buffalo, carved from green quartzite. Carvings such as this express the reverence for, and the desire to be connected with, important hunt animals, such as the buffalo.

Shoshone hide painting depicting a buffalo dance after the hunt. Hunting buffalo was often very risky and a successful hunt was considered a great blessing to the People, who celebrated accordingly.

But why was hunting so dangerous? Of course, the animals themselves could be hard to kill, and if only wounded, could turn upon the hunter: Imagine an angry buffalo bearing down on you at full speed. Other reasons are more curious and are closely related to the stories or myths told by individual tribes. Sometimes it was told that animals were kept imprisoned by powerful chiefs or spirits or monsters, hidden away from the world and the hungry people looking for them. In such cases, the hunter would have to undertake a dangerous journey to the land of the Animal Keeper. Only after the Animal Keeper was defeated would the animals be released and the hunter return to his people with food.

The Comanche tell of a time when two Old People, two Ancient Ones, were the Animal Keepers and owned all the buffalo. All the buffalo were kept locked away in the mountains so that they could not escape, and no other people could find them. It was at this time that Coyote helped the People by tricking the Animal Keepers. Coyote sent a small animal to the place where the buffalo were kept. The Old People kept the small animal as a pet. But when night came, the little creature began to howl. This noise frightened the buffalo and they charged the gate, broke it down, and escaped out onto the land. The next morning, all the hungry people mounted their horses; they knew Coyote had helped them. They hunted the buffalo from that day forward. This is how buffalo came to live on the land and how Coyote once helped the People with his trickery.

RESPECTING THE ANIMALS

The hunter had to be in the right frame of mind for the hunt to be successful. The hunter needed to be respectful of the animal spirits so they would offer themselves. A hunter had to be careful. Careful in his mind, careful in his actions. The moment the hunter became careless was when the trouble started.

Even though animals were hunted for food, people still needed to respect them. Without respect, the animals would not allow themselves to be taken. It was important not to take more than was needed. Lack of respect could have dangerous consequences, as this story from the Yaudanchi people of California relates . . .

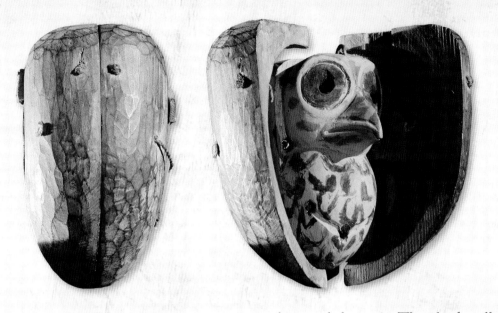

A heart-shaped charm of the Tsimshian tribe, which, when opened, reveals an owl representing the soul of one who recently died. In some tribes, owls carry powerful medicine, feared by some, revered by others.

AT THAT TIME, a man was traveling with his wife. They had walked a very great distance, so when night came, they decided to rest in a cave. There was no food there. They had traveled far. There was no food and they were hungry. They started a fire. As they sat at their fire, they heard a calling at the mouth of the cave. This was the hoot of Hutulu, the horned owl. The wife had an idea. "Call back to the owl," she said to her husband. "Perhaps he will come closer and you can shoot him." The man followed his wife's advice. He called to the owl. The owl called back. Again and again they called to each other, each time the owl moving a little closer to the cave. The man got his bow and arrows ready. When the owl could be seen at the mouth of the cave, the man took careful aim and shot it.

"Do this again," his wife told him. "Call to the owls again and another one will come." Again, the man did as his wife told him. Soon another owl was in sight. He shot this one as well. "Good," the man said, "this is enough."

But his wife told him to call again. She told him that they would want more meat in the morning, and the owls would not answer him that early in the day. Why not take more at night, when the owls are in abundance and will answer no matter how many times you call them?

So the man called again. The owls came. So many of them! They did not stop. He shot at many, until his arrows were gone, but more kept coming. The man and his wife could not count so many owls. All at once, the owls attacked. The man covered his wife with a basket to protect her. He took burning branches from the fire to try to scare the owls away. But there were too many owls. Soon, the man and his wife were killed. It is not good to take too many. This is how the owls were avenged upon the greedy couple. ☀

Stories such as this one have important messages for both ancient times as well as today. How often do we take more than we need? It is important to realize that natural resources are limited. We must remember that there are consequences of taking too much from the land without showing the proper respect.

THE HUNT FOR KNOWLEDGE

Hunters were often heroes because they brought food to the tribe. But food was not the only thing worth hunting. There are other kinds of heroes as well: women and men who, through their journeys and experiences, bring knowledge to their people.

Sometimes journeys were undertaken to bring back special or magical objects. Other times, it was only the journey itself that was important. In many tribes, people will undertake the quest for a vision when they are at a crossroads in their lives. This quest can take many forms, but often requires the person to make a special journey, or pilgrimage out into the land. While on this journey, spirits may be encountered, animals seen, or important information received through dreams and visions.

Used on the prow of a large Tlingit war canoe, this figure of Land-Otter-Man is pointing ahead to indicate the safest direction for the hunters in the canoe to take. Land-Otter-Man's association with the sea was established in Tlingit mythology, in which he rescues the souls of drowning people and turns them into land otters.

Long ago among the Winnebago people, a young man went into the hills to fast and pray. After going without food for twelve days, he had a vision in which a spirit came to him. This spirit had been sent by the Earth Maker to give the young man knowledge and powerful words that would bring health, luck, and long life. For many long nights that spirit called up songs for the young man and told him many things that would help the People. When that young man left the hills, he was very wise. Upon his return to his people, he shared his knowledge with them, teaching them wonderful songs, just as the spirit had taught them to him. These songs are powerful and secret, and are still used by the Winnebago in their medicine ceremonies.

Of course, not all journeys are undertaken for sacred purposes. Some people may undertake journeys for the simplest reason of all: curiosity. They wish to see what there is to see just beyond the next hill, or over the far river, or at the end of the long trail leading toward dawn . . .

The Journey to Dawn
(Cherokee)

At that time, among the Cherokee people, there were some curious folks. Several brave young people decided they wanted to see the place of the sunrise and perhaps look upon the sun himself. They packed things they would need for a long journey: weapons, extra clothing, parched corn for food.

They traveled to the east and met many people on their way. The first people were people they knew, their neighbors. Then they met people they had heard about from the stories of traveling traders. At last they met people of whom they had never heard tell: These were strange people with languages

LEFT: Inuit socks braided from grass, worn to absorb perspiration and hence reduce the impact of frostbite. Every part of a journey is important—even the smallest objects that accompany one are worthy of time, craft, and detail.

OPPOSITE: Plains war club. The handle is wrapped with bearskin and human hair.

and customs very different from their own. The travelers did not stay long in those strange lands.

On and on they walked until they came to the place where the sky reaches the ground. Here they found the place of sunrise and learned that the sky was an arch of rock, always swinging above the earth. When it swung up, there was an entrance place between the earth and sky. It was from this entrance that the sun came into the world and, walking along the inside of the arch, made the daytime. The sun was bright and hot, too hot to approach, but the People could see that he had a human shape.

The travelers knew they had come to the end of the world and decided to turn back. But they had traveled for a very long time indeed, and when they returned to their village, they had all become old and many of the People they knew as youths had passed away. The journey did not seem long, but in truth, they had been gone for many, many years—many turnings of the sun beneath his arch of stone.

RAIDING AND WARFARE

Many journeys began at first light. But other journeys started quietly, under shadow of night.

ONCE, A RAIDING PARTY moved across the dark plains. They had become shadows, running, then crawling, toward an enemy camp. They had come for horses. They wanted to be heroes. Their journey home was much shorter, for now they were riding. When their enemies awoke and found their horses stolen, they pursued the raiding party and fought bravely for what was theirs. And now, this night, we will follow such a trail and take back what is ours and more.

Crow pipe. During times of war, the leader of a Crow war party would regularly sit apart from the others and smoke a pipe in an attempt to establish communion with the Sacred Powers whose advice he sought. Horse hooves on the bowl of this pipe indicate that it was used during horse raids.

Battles between villages and sometimes whole tribes often followed such activities. Yet war and fighting could have other purposes. Fighting proved bravery and won honor for the warrior and his family. Men of all ages took part in such battles. Boys were raised believing that to die defending your people was a noble deed. They did not fear death. Among the Plains cultures (the Lakota, Cheyenne, Crow, Pawnee, and others) it was not always even necessary to kill an enemy. Objects were used, called *coup* sticks. These were used to strike an enemy, but not kill him. If you could touch an enemy and walk or ride away, it was a great honor, as the risk to one's life was so great.

Because the road to war almost always required a long journey to another land, there are many songs and magical charms associated with battle and protection when traveling far from home. When the warrior encountered hardships, a special song could restore his bravery and help put him back upon the right path.

YOU, wide arc of the blue sky,
You see me wandering upon my road;
On the path of war I am wandering, lonely.
In you I place my trust, protect and guide me!
    —*Coyote warrior song, Pawnee*

Fox (tribe) necklace with a matched row of grizzly bear claws worn as a mark of distinction. Trophies won in a hunt could also convey power and authority during times of war.

Before setting out on the road to war, ceremonies were held to bless the warriors. Upon their return, more songs were sung to celebrate victory, or to praise the bravery of comrades who were slain. A Cheyenne song speaks of rejoicing while taunting those who did not go to war, did not paint their faces black for battle, but remained at home:

> WHO are these
> Who stand and gaze at us?
> Who are these
> With red paint thick upon them?
> By day, in the sight of all men
> We charged to war!

THE FINAL JOURNEY

There is a journey that awaits us all. But very few people return to tell of it. When death comes, for some, the road to the Otherworld is long and filled with difficulty. For others, death is merely a change of country and landscape. Each Native American tribe has its own beliefs about death and the Otherworld.

Kwakiutl skull masks, used in traditional dance ceremonies. Symbols of death help people accept the idea of death.

Among the tribes of the Northwest coast, the dead live in villages far from the lands of the living. Living people have traveled to these villages, and some have returned to tell the tale: The houses appeared very richly adorned, the dead were likewise dressed in beautiful clothes. But this was an illusion. When the living visitors looked more closely, they found the villages were in ruins and the inhabitants were skeletons who could walk and speak. Upon seeing such frightening sights, living visitors to the Otherworld might decide that staying close to home was a better idea.

In the Southeast, among tribes such as the Cherokee and Natchez, there were many beliefs about how the dead should be treated. It is believed that the spirit or soul of the deceased lived on after death, and that the dead person's wishes must be attended to. In ancient times, there were elaborate rituals for the dead. Sometimes, after the body had lain out upon a platform, or been buried in the ground, it would be removed, the bones cleaned and placed in a special temple. If the wishes of the dead were not respected, it could be dangerous for the living.

Even under the best of circumstances, there were no guarantees that the dead would be kind to the living. Sometimes they hung around and caused trouble. Among the Navajo, the ghost of the deceased, called *chi'ndii*, would remain around the place of death, its family, or its former home. In such cases, the journey after death would be taken by the deceased person's surviving family, for the survivors would move away from the house where the person had died. If someone died in the hogan (a traditional Navajo dwelling), the north wall would be broken out, and the family would abandon that place. The ruins of such homes can still be seen off the backroads in Arizona and New Mexico—broken, often burned, lonely places, haunted by the past.

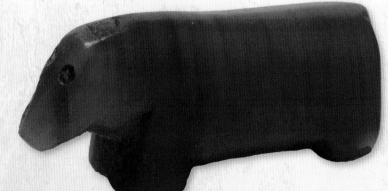

LEFT: Carried in a pouch or, later, a pocket, small charms like this twentieth-century Navajo horse carving kept a traveler safe upon his or her journey.

OPPOSITE: Shattering the common stereotype of Southeastern tribes as peaceful farmers, gorgets such as this tell a different story: an intensely ranked society in which violence and warfare were a part of life.

THE POWER OF RETURNING AND TELLING

When a person sets out upon a journey—whether to hunt for food or knowledge, to make war, or even to visit the Otherworld—they are never the same when they return. Traveling changes us. Journeys shape our memories and expand our experiences. Those things we bring back from the hunt—either food or knowledge—sustain us and keep us curious about the world.

Think of your own travels and adventures out upon the land or in foreign countries: What wonderful stories do you have to tell? What experiences have you "hunted" or sought on your travels? What have you learned from the land? The stories told *about* journeys are as important (perhaps more important) than the destination. The journey lasts for a only a fixed time, but the stories told of it, the wisdom brought back, can keep traveling forever, keep living, even after the tellers have traveled on.

AT THAT TIME, in the West, the Earth opened its mouth. The great jaws of the Earth stretched apart and the People wandered out and settled nearby. But the Earth was angry, angry with the People, and so began eating their children. Mourning their losses, the People began to walk—farther and farther West they went. Some didn't care for traveling, didn't care for the new lands, so they returned to that place where they were before and settled there again. Many returned, and as before, their children were eaten by the Earth. Finally, they knew they could not stay in that place. Full of sadness, full of regret, they journeyed toward the place where the sun fell.   —*Creek*

Dark Dance of the Little People by W. Richard West, Sr. (WAH-PAH-NAH-YAH, Cheyenne), 1948.

CHAPTER SIX

Little People
The Eyes of the Forest

The Lost Ones

In bits of frozen stars,
hung in the soft
velvet blanket
shrouding the
cold dark air,
we reach toward
bright sparkling lights.
This is the place
we breathe,
singing
the songs of the night.
Can you hear
the sounds of the
turtle shell rattles,
ashes and stars
singing upon the
breeze of remembering?
Our hair is long,
fingernails too,

antlers rise
like mist upon water.
We rise,
singing,
and we know
the call of the night,
like we know
our blood.

Ogla chahta homa
They are red.
Wandering into the woods
they come,
called by the songs
sung by the turtle.
Laughter reminds them
of the dreams
of children,
when mother's kiss

called them home.
We are here to greet them,
with songs and stars
and red earth of home,
mother's kisses
and turtle shell rattles.
This now becomes home
while the world moves
on around them.
Years later
seeming only days,
they return to a home
that is no longer their own.
Humming songs and looking
    lost,
children singing songs
from mouths
of the long dead.

Nearly every country in the world has stories of "little people." North American Indian tribes are no exception, and while rare, stories of fairy- or dwarflike creatures inhabiting out-of-the-way places are still told. Many tribes consider them to be human beings, only very small in size. Some people believe them to be powerful spirits that watch humans to ensure that proper codes of conduct (or special behaviors) are being followed. Whether human or spirits, the Little People are mostly encountered at night, living in caves or burrows in the ground during the day. Rarely seen, their footsteps may be heard in the forests if all is very quiet.

Mostly, these stories are found in parts of North America where there are large forests, deep woods, or wide tracks of unspoiled wilderness, although, like the little people themselves, such tales can spring up in the most unlikely places. Even the People of the Arctic tell of such creatures.

A CURIOUS FAMILY

Now, if you found yourself walking far out upon the northern tundra, you might see a very curious family. The man might be so small that he is dressed in a coat made from the skin of only one white fox. The woman's clothes would be fashioned from the skins of two small white hares. And their child? Why, two muskrat furs would be all that was needed to keep him warm. Deer hunters have seen the tracks of such people, but they are seldom found. They are quick to frighten, and can vanish quickly into the ground. It has been a very long time since anyone has spoken to one of these Little People, but the Inuit know that they are harmless and have never hurt anyone.

GUARDIANS OF THE WILD PLACES

Some Southeastern tribes believe that in order to see the Little People, a person must fast (go without food) for a certain number of days and make a journey to their land in the company of a medicine man. For the most part, however, it was better to leave the Little People to themselves.

In some Southeastern traditions, Little People are like other folk: humans, only smaller. But there are also spirits that take the shape of Little People. One such group of spirits is called Yunwitsandsdi by the Cherokee. These spirits live among the rocks and hillside caves of northern Georgia and the Carolinas.

The Yunwitsandsdi are great lovers of music. Sometimes, deep in the woods or in the mountains, the sound of drums can be heard. It is best not to follow the sound, however. While these spirits are usually helpful and kind, they do not like unwanted visitors and have been known to cast spells over unwelcome guests. Unlucky people can become lost in the wilderness, some never returning to their homes. The Little People can also be of great help if asked.

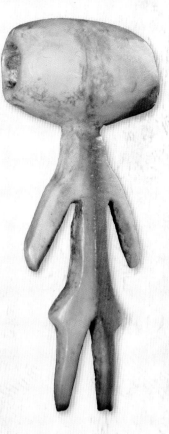

ABOVE: Inuit ivory bead or pendant carved in semi-human form, northern Canada. Not all Little People are necessarily miniature versions of human beings; they are spirits and may adopt many forms.

OPPOSITE: Lush rain forest bordering Prince William Sound, near Inuit country. Stories of Little People are more often than not stories about the wild places in the world.

Red argillite pendant, Sinagua, northwestern Arizona. Representations of birds take many forms in art and artifacts and can sometimes hold similar meanings in tribes of the various regions.

The Daughter of Sun

Now, Sun lived on one side of the sky, and her daughter lived on the other, and every day Sun would stop, at a certain time of the day, and visit Redbird, her daughter, for dinner.

Sun became very angry with the People, because when the People would look at her they would hide their eyes, screw them shut, and try to look away. Sun believed the People thought her ugly, and said to her brother, Moon, "My grandchildren are ugly. When they look at me, their faces are grimaced and silly. I don't like the way they look at me," to which Moon replied, "I think they are beautiful. They always look upon me with longing and are very handsome." This made Sun even more angry, because she knew the People thought her brother was better-looking, and she was jealous. She decided to kill the People. Every day as she reached her Redbird's house in the middle of the sky, Sun would shine bright, hot rays upon the People, scorching them and drying out the land. There was a great fever and many people were dying—so many that soon there would be no one left. So it was that the medicine people turned to the Little People, the Yunwitsandsdi, for help.

The Yunwitsandsdi made medicine and turned two men into snakes. They sent the two snakes, Adder and Copperhead, to bite old Sun when she came to her daughter's house. But when Sun left her daughter's house, her beauty was so great and hot that it blinded the snakes and they could only spit in Sun's direction. When Sun saw this, she laughed and called out, "You silly creatures, step away from me!" The two snakes, outdone by her, slithered off.

More people died of the fever, and the medicine people went back to the Little People for help. The Little People changed two more men into snakes, Diamond Back and Uktena. Now, both of these snakes were very crafty. Uktena had horns on his head and Diamond Back coiled quickly, ready to strike. The Little People thought that Uktena, the Snake-man, with his terrible horns and long fangs, would certainly kill Sun as she left Redbird's house, but it was Diamond Back who eagerly coiled in the dry bushes and who struck first when the door opened. However Diamond Back's fangs didn't sink into Sun's bright fire, but into the red flesh of Redbird, killing her instantly.

When Sun came and found Redbird dead, she went into her daughter's house and grieved heavily. The People weren't dying from heat anymore, but from cold and wind because Sun wouldn't come out of Redbird's house. So the medicine people went back to the Yunwitsandsdi and begged for their help. The Yunwitsandsdi told the medicine

Plains—possibly Shoshone—beaded buckskin pouch in the form of a snake. Such pouches contained a baby's umbilical cord and were fastened to the front of cradles as "playthings" for their occupants. They were worn later in life as charms to avert ill health and ensure long life. As representations of the sky, lightning, and earth, snakes are never to be underestimated—as in nature—in any stories where they're found.

LEFT: Two Eastern woodlands pipe bowls from the early ninth century, one in the form of a kneeling human figure, the other an animal with a beak and prominent ears. Small objects such as these found on the land are often thought to be made by Little People or other spirits.

OPPOSITE: Small flints and arrowheads are often evidence of the Little People's presence.

people that if they wanted Sun to stop her grief then they must go to the Ghost Country and bring the daughter back, so Sun would find joy again. The medicine people chose seven men from each clan to go to the Ghost Country, and there the men would find the daughter of Sun, Redbird, dancing with the other spirits. Each of the men were given a walking stick by the Yunwitsandsdi. With these sticks they were to touch the daughter of Sun until she fell to the ground. Then they were to put her in a cane basket and bring her back to Sun. But, the Yunwitsandsdi warned, do not let Redbird out of the basket, no matter what she says or does, or else all will be lost.

As they came to the Ghost Country, the seven men did what they were told, each striking Redbird until she fell, and placing her in the basket given to them by the Yunwitsandsdi. They then led her away, the other ghosts unaware of her disappearance. The further from the Ghost Country the men got, the louder the wailing came from the basket. The daughter of Sun cried so loud, asking for water, for air, for food . . . but the men kept on with their task. Soon, Redbird, the daughter of Sun, cried louder and louder, that she couldn't breathe in the basket and surely she would die without air. So the men stopped and opened the basket a little, and as they did a fluttering sound came out of the basket—"kwish, kwish"—and they saw a redbird fly above them. When they got back home, they found the basket empty.

Sun saw the empty basket and cried and cried, knowing Redbird was gone forever. Soon, floods appeared and people were truly suffering. The medicine men went to the Yunwitsandsdi again, and this time the Little People told them to dance for Sun, sing for her, and pray for her. And so they did, singing to Sun, dancing for her, praying for her. Gradually, Sun began to hear the songs of the People, and soon her grief subsided. She looked down, and was pleased with the beauty of the People, and smiled. ☀

Sometimes, objects are found in the forest, perhaps a flint knife or a small carving. If this happens, the person who finds the object must ask permission of the Yunwitsandsdi to keep it, because it probably belongs to one of the Little People. He must call to the Little People, saying, "I want to keep this." If the finder does not ask their permission, bad luck could befall him, and the Yunwitsandsdi might throw stones at him all the way home.

Usually though, the Yunwitsandsdi are very kind and most of the stories told about them speak of their rescuing lost children by caring for them in the wilderness and then bringing them back to their homes.

Not all of the Little People are so kind, however. They can play tricks on people and make them lose their way in the wilderness. Among some California tribes, Little Folk called *Sè-kah* live in deep redwood forests where no people travel or live. It is believed that seeing them could cause madness.

The Cherokee also speak of another kind of Little People who live in Tullulah Gorge, in what is now northern Georgia. Many hunters have been lost in this place, for the tiny folk who inhabit it do not like visitors. Even powerful medicine men could not drive the Little People away, and so that land is no longer hunted and people enter the gorge at their peril.

THE *NIMMIMBE*

The Shoshone people of the Great Basin and Wyoming know that when ancient dwellings are found in remote regions, great care must be taken. These structures, built from mud, sticks, and stones are the homes of the *Ninnimbe*, the Little People, or "little demons."

The *Ninnimbe* are no more than three feet tall. They wear clothing made of mountain sheep skin and are known for their strength and great courage. They are clever hunters and walk the land with quivers that are always full of arrows. These arrows are poisoned and often invisible. If you look carefully around ruins and ancient piles of stones, small arrowheads may be found that, it is believed, were made by the *Ninnimbe* long ago.

If any bad luck befalls a person, it is often blamed on the *Ninnimbe*. If a person's horse goes lame, or someone becomes sick, or if accidents happen when one is setting out upon a journey, it could be that the *Ninnimbe* have been offended.

In the Wind River country of Wyoming, there are many drawings made on the rocks. It is thought that the *Ninnimbe* made these images and that it brings bad luck to look upon them for too long. On rare dark nights, these drawings speak amongst themselves. What they say to each other, what stories they tell in the shadow-time before dawn, are not known.

If in the middle of the night strange, small sounds are heard, it is thought that one of the *Ninnimbe* is trying to catch people while they sleep. When this happens, the fearful person creeps away to the hills or canyons or some deserted place, hoping to hide from his pursuer. When he returns at dawn, he will walk as quietly as possible so that the *Ninnimbe* will not be able to follow him home. This is how it was always done, since the earliest times.

ABOVE: Rio Grande petroglyphs from the Pueblo region of New Mexico.

OPPOSITE: Petroglyphs from the Wind River region of Wyoming. Many of the images are recognizable as animals, people, brands and crosses, while others are more complex and are thought to have had religious meaning. Depictions of Spirit People and spirits, found on rocks, may embody warnings that no one is alone even in the wilderness.

A LITTLE MAGIC

Elements of magic are common to most Native American stories of Little People. These creatures are often powerful magicians and can cast spells over people for good or ill purposes, depending on the circumstances. Usually, the Little People are guardians of the animals, or certain places in the land, like woods, caves, or rivers. When crossing the borders into lands inhabited by the Little People, special rules have to be observed, and special care needs to be taken so that they are not offended.

The Little People's magic could be worked on humans in interesting ways, and sometimes, very kindly. A young girl of the Northeastern Miqmaq tribe was bathing in the river when a tiny canoe with a tiny man in it came paddling close to her. The

girl picked up the canoe in her hand and took it home with her. She was told by her parents to take the little man back to the river. This she did, but not before making friends with him. The little man promised to return one day to visit the young girl. Every day, she returned to the river, looking for her friend.

A long time passed, and one day this girl was picking berries with some other children. Then, she noticed a dozen little canoes coming swiftly down the river toward her. The canoe leading the others was paddled by the little man she had met some years ago. As it happens, he was the chief of a tribe of Little People. The canoes landed, and the Little People prepared a meal. When the meal was done, the little man said to the Miqmaq girls, "If you would like to travel to the other side of the river, we shall take you in our canoes." Well, the girls laughed and laughed at this idea. How could they fit into such tiny little canoes? The chief of the Little People told the girl to try, and no sooner had she put one toe into the tiny canoe, then she became tiny as well. She persuaded the other children to step into canoes, and soon they all were upon the water, paddling toward the far shore in the little canoes. As soon as they reached the shore and the children stepped out of the canoes, they were back to normal size. The little chief, wishing them farewell, returned to the river and was not seen again, but the story of the Little People's visit has been told ever since.

MANY NAMES

The Little People are known by as many names as there are tribes to name them . . .

Apicilnic are known among the Montagnais of Labrador. The sight of these Little People portends danger, for they sometimes steal children away from their families.

Djigaahehwa are helpful to the Iroquois of the Northeast, and help medicinal plants to grow.

Lawalawa are small creatures who live in the wilderness surrounding the Coos people of the Northwest. These troublesome neighbors are also called the "noisy ones" because they spend their time throwing rocks at people's houses. They are great wrestlers and are not afraid of challenging big people. Their tracks can often be found along creek beds and streams.

And there are many, many more, for every land has its secrets.

Whether helpful or mischievous, kind or dangerous, Little People and the stories told about them remind us to be careful in the wilderness, to keep our eyes open. Stories of Little People embody many mysteries. What happens to powerful stories when only parts of them are remembered? Does the passing of years and the rare mentioning of their names make gods and spirits smaller? What shapes are taken by these small but powerful spirits of the woods and wild places of the land? Are there truly Little People hiding in and protecting the lonely corners of the world? Will they help or hinder us?

Such stories ask us to remember that there are little things in the world around us that we hardly notice but which contain great beauty and strength; that we might learn by taking a closer look at places we already thought we knew; that we overlook important knowledge by not asking enough questions of the land around us; that some places in the wilderness are not for us to visit; that there are always small, secret wonders hiding in nature, just out of view.

OPPOSITE, TOP: Mojave child's doll, southern California. Children, in particular, seem prone to encounter Little People. Often Little People will help them return home safely. All children who go wandering in the wilderness are not that lucky. Those who are not found by the Little People may never find their way home. For this reason, the Little People who guard the deep places of the world must always be shown respect.

OPPOSITE, BOTTOM: Inuit plug from a drag float, carved in ivory in the form of a feminine human face, Alaska. Drag floats, which were attached to harpoons when hunting walrus and seals in open water, were made from the skin of a seal that was inflated by blowing through a mouthpiece capped with a plug. Something very small yet very useful, the plug is a reminder that things of beauty can come in many forms and sizes.

Untitled by Fred Kabotie (Hopi), 1922.

CHAPTER SEVEN

Tricksters & Transformations

Animal Tales

Deer Woman

The woman who is a deer
    followed me home,
through deep, dark woods.
Forests abundant with
bright greens, reds, Earth browns
and dark, daylit skies.
There and back, to this place
    of stars and light
and now she's not
about to let go.
She speaks in deer tongues, upon
hooves of steel and glass,
concrete and sand,
of myth and forgiveness
but the truth sits on
my tongue

waiting to fly
. . . a deer tongue on a salt lick.
How can she sing a song
to call the deer home?
I am home, I said,
    in this place of angels
and stars.
She laughs,
thinks it ironic
after all this time
you got what you wanted.
Did you not see the flash of hoof
on a dark moonlit road
hear me whisper stars in your ear?
You see, my girl, the trick is this:
    bewitch their spirit

so when their soul comes along
they have no home left to
bear down their spirit
with my teeth
soft voice
words of darkness,
their blood my water
I leave you now

a deer
a woman
missing the trees that call your heart
and I follow the deer
across the field map of stars
to the place she calls
home.

Calusa deer head ceremonial
carving, from south Florida.
Representations of clan totems
often appear as carvings in
stone or wood and as masks in
Southeastern ritual art.

As we grow up, everybody hears the same thing from the grown-ups in their lives. "Don't talk with your mouth full of food," "Don't put your elbows on the table," "Don't sing during dinner," and "Don't walk over puddles after the rain because the Water Panther might reach up from under the ground and get you!"

Maybe sometimes Grandma just doesn't want you to get wet and cold. But there's always a story behind the story. That's how the story never ends: Someone is always telling it, someone is always listening. A story is told about something someone else did once so that we won't make that same mistake now.

This is a story Grandma told a long time ago.

The Boy Who Was
(Choctaw)

Two young men were hunting. One belonged to the Deer Clan, the ones who make songs of light and send them to the stars. The other belonged to the clan that is related to the Hawk, the messengers, the ones who stay silent and speak only when the world must be spoken to.

They had been hunting a long time, singing the charm songs they had been taught, the songs to hunt for a deer, to woo a deer. They had seen the antlers hiding in shadow, hiding in sunlight, along the oily leaves and sweet-scented magnolia, along the light pathways, in the darkness of the fireflies, and hidden in soft wood, water, damp bark. They heard the deer sing, and could have sworn it was the voice of a woman.

The two men, barely out of their youth, turned to one another, and began to sing their hunting songs louder. Surely, this was no male deer, but with antlers? They had become separated from the rest of the hunting party and knew they would be lost at once if they did not perform the ceremony for hunting the deer. One reached for the dark earth and put it to his face, singing a charm song all the way. *Brother deer,* he sang, *sister fawn, blood of my blood, there is nothing to fear from me. Let my arrows be strong, may they find your heart. Do not fear.*

The other, with steady hands, made fire.

The fire carried an ascent of prayers to the darkening sky. A cool wind rose off the river and soon seeped into the gaps between the clothing of the hunters. The fire was warm, but their bellies were empty. As the one who sang the charm song continued his prayer, the other looked and saw in a clearing near the water three small eggs. Cracking the eggs into the fire, he cooked them and prepared to divide them with his companion. "Where did these come from?" The one who sang the song asked.

"They were here, at this camp," said the one who had cooked.

"Who has laid them?" asked the one who sang.

His companion replied, "They were here in camp, waiting for us to eat."

"I will not eat what I do not know," the one who sang said.

His companion was hungry and ready to eat the eggs. On the first bite, the eggs slid down his throat and into his empty belly. They were light as air, and tasted of smoke and fire and water and life. They filled him, and he craved more.

The one who sang stoked the fire. "The deer will surely show himself tonight," he said, "and I must stay and watch for him. You sleep."

And his companion did, and all night he dreamt of water and wood. In his dream, his hands and feet would not move. He woke, feverish, his companion keeping watch over him. "My hands . . ." he whispered, and could not move them.
The one who sang moved closer. "You should not have eaten those eggs," he said, concerned for his friend. "You are having trouble now. Go to sleep, and soon you will awaken and the illness will pass."

And sleep he did, but his dreams were even more fitful and frightening. In his dreams, his feet and legs were numb, and he could not move. When he woke, his fevered cries brought the alarmed attention of his companion. "It is the eggs," his friend said. "Go and sleep the sickness away."

And he dreamt again, of the world beneath this one, of a world of coldness and dark, of vast underground tunnels that led from this world to the world of the spirits. And he was frightened because he could see into both worlds, and he knew that something was happening to him, something that had been set into motion that he could not control.

He woke, unable to move. His hands and feet had grown together, seamless. His friend looked upon him in horror. "Go. Find the village. Find my family," the one who ate the eggs implored his friend. "They will help me."

The one who sang ran through the woods, and to his surprise, soon found himself at the village. He rounded up his friend's family as well as his own, running back to the place by the river. All that was left was a skin shed by a snake and a trail leading to the river. ☀

This was the story our grandma used to tell us, and we tell it now, so that we never forget that dark things may dwell below the surface of the water. We never forget where we came from, who we are, and why we're not supposed to step over puddles after the rain—whatever might lie beneath them.

Has an animal ever "spoken" to you? Do you ever feel like an animal? Brave as a lion? Quick as a rabbit? Slow as a turtle? People have always felt strong associations with animals. Sometimes, we use common animal traits to help explain our own feelings and experiences; for example, "stubborn as a mule." In the Native American tradition, people and animals are even more closely related. People don't just imagine they have animal traits. Sometimes, through magic, they can become animals.

In many tribal stories, people are related to animals in the same manner they are related to their cousins, sisters, brothers, mothers, and fathers. Specific groups within individual tribes, called clans, are often named for animals because those people are descended from a common ancestor who might be Raven, Badger, Bear, Eagle, or other animals. Those animals share a vital role in that clan's history and experience and help to define them as a people.

Kosimo Kwakiutl house post carved to represent the "speaker" of the house, Quatsino Sound, Alaska. On the Northwest coast, clans and ancestors are often represented by animals from which they are descended.

ORIGINS

Everything has an origin. Just as the world itself had a beginning, so did all the things in it, and animals are no exception to this. Any one creature may have many different stories told about it. In addition to stories about how each animal came to be, each tribe has a collection of myths that explain why animals do what they do. Often, these stories also have something to say about the origins of animals, that is, how each animal came to take its place in the world. Usually, these places are chosen by gods, but every now and then, the animals got to choose for themselves.

How the Animals Chose Their Places
(Northern Paiute)

Coyote was in charge in those days.

He said to Bear, "Perhaps you should stay in those mountains."

Well, now Deer liked that idea and wanted to live in the mountains too.

Then Whitefish spoke up saying, "I need water."

"Yes!" said Duck, "Water sounds pretty good."

Then Swan started looking at himself, "Look how white I'm becoming. Look how pretty I am."

Bear began to hit the ground and said, "Ground, tell me who is saying things about me."

Ground said, "Well, that person over there isn't saying anything nice."

Bear went right over to that person and gave him a bite.

ABOVE: Images such as the standing bear on this Plains Indian shield were often created to convey both human and animal traits, emphasizing the important relationship between animals and humans.

OPPOSITE: *Wolf Warrior* by Samuel Banagas (Luiseno), 1987. Stories of shape-shifting humans and animals abound in Native America and can represent not only the connectedness between humans and animal spirits but also the everyday interdependence of humans and animals.

Mountain Sheep jumped up then and said he liked
    the rocks and high places. He would stay there.
Rock said he like being close to the ground. Rock
    wanted to stay in one place and not have to
    move around.
Some plants agreed with Rock. So they stayed
    put too.
This is how it all came about.

TRANSFORMATION

In the early days following Creation, there was
only a thin line (if any at all) between humans and
animals. In those mythic times, the shapes of things
were not set. Animals could become people; people
could become animals, and animals could even
become other animals. Even now, it is known that
through magic, people and animals can change
their shapes and become like one another.

Transformation can happen in many ways. Sometimes, the change from human to
animal is an accident, or partly an accident. The Inuit of the lower Yukon tell of a little
girl who lived in a village by the river. Someone used magic to change her into a bird
with a long beak. When the change took place she became very frightened, and when
she tried to fly away, her flying was poor and she rolled this way and that way in the air.
Finally, she flew into the side of a house and this shortened her beak and face so that she
took the form of the short-eared owl.

Some people, like the Owl Girl, remained in animal shape for the rest of their lives.
Other people could change back and forth at will. In Labrador, Canada, there are stories
of Fox Woman, who could be a human one moment but then put on her other skin and
become a fox just as easily.

Though it is a rare thing, animals could even take the shape of other animals. The
Wichita people have told of a time when Coyote wanted to become a buffalo.

Coyote Becomes a Buffalo

Now, Coyote saw how well the buffalo were eating, and he wished to eat the same way, by wandering about grazing. Finally, Coyote asked one of the buffalo if he could become like them. Buffalo thought about it for a long time, but finally told Coyote that if he were brave, he could become a buffalo, for only the bravest people could be buffalo. Of course, Coyote told Buffalo that he was the bravest person who ever lived. No lie.

Buffalo told Coyote to walk a distance away. He told Coyote that he would run at him, would run him down, but when Coyote got back up, he would indeed be a buffalo. Three times, Coyote got scared and stepped out of the way. But on the fourth try, Coyote closed his eyes and held his ground. Buffalo ran him over, and when Coyote stood up again, he had become a buffalo.

Arapaho painted buffalo skull. Buffalo is a holy animal, thought by some Plains tribes to be the living shadow of the sun. Buffalo are an important source of food and other resources; even the skulls of the buffalo are revered and hold, among Plains tribes, an important place in the Sun Dance ceremony.

Now Coyote-Buffalo was very pleased with himself and went about eating and drinking as buffalo do. This went on for some time. One day, Coyote-Buffalo met another coyote. He told that coyote that he could make him a buffalo too. Well, that sounded pretty good to that coyote. So things happened as before, and every time Coyote-Buffalo ran at the other coyote, that coyote got scared and stepped out of the way. But the fourth time, that coyote stood still and Coyote-Buffalo knocked him to the ground. But when Coyote-Buffalo ran Coyote down, they both cried, in the manner of coyotes. And they were both coyotes again instead of buffalo. But this is always what happened to Coyote in those days. When he was given medicine by other animals, something always went wrong and he ended up right back where he started.

Hohokam pigment mortar in the form of a horned toad, Arizona, early tenth century. Even the smallest animals have lessons to impart and are considered both kin and neighbors. Their appearance in art and ritual objects attests to these close connections.

LEARNING FROM ANIMALS

One of the reasons people and animals share such a close relationship is that people have always learned important lessons from animals: what to eat, and what not to eat; when it is safe, or when there is danger about.

Have you ever walked in a park or a forest where there were no birds singing and no small animals to be seen? It's unsettling, isn't it? Where have the birds gone? And why did they leave? Often, animals can warn us of trouble before we are able to detect it ourselves. Many people have been saved from fires by their pets, who, sensing the danger early, woke their owners and allowed them to get to safety. By carefully watching animals and their behavior, people can learn, and have learned, a great deal about their environment.

Some animals can teach us a lot about survival. The tribes of the North have always watched polar bears to see where the best hunting is, because polar bears are such exceptional hunters. The Inuit call him He Who Has No Shadow, because the polar bear never lets its prey know that it is approaching. By watching the bear hunt, the Inuit learned vital techniques for surviving in their harsh Arctic environment.

Even small animals can be helpful. Once, two hunters were making their dinner at their small camp, deep in the forest. As they ate they heard the song of the katydid. One of the hunters made fun of the little insect and said how sad it was that the katydid went on singing when it didn't know that it would die before the end of the season. But Katydid spoke to them and said that the hunter should not be so proud, for tomorrow, his own death awaited him. Well, this hunter did not heed Katydid's warning, and the next day, the man was killed by an enemy. Perhaps if he had not been so proud and had listened to Katydid's omen, he would be here now, telling his own story.

TRICKSTERS

But the examples set by animals are not always to be followed. Sometimes, certain animals, like Coyote, would teach people proper behavior by always doing the wrong things—by tricking people, and getting in trouble for it. Sometimes, these stories simply tell how one animal did something clever or unpleasant to another, which resulted in changing that animal's appearance, or everyone learning an important lesson. The animals in these kinds of situations have been called tricksters, and there are many stories about them in the Native American tradition. These stories are extremely important because they set up standards for proper behavior as well as telling us how certain things (an animal's appearance, fire, or certain rules) came about. People listen to these stories, learn from the mistakes of animals like Coyote, and know how to behave in the future in order to avoid trouble.

Rabbit Steals Fire
(Creek)

There was a time when people did not have fire. Everyone got to together to try to think of a way to get it, because fire was sacred and had so many uses. After many long discussions, it was decided that Rabbit should be the one to try to get fire for the People.

Rabbit traveled far to the east, across the great water. There he was received by people he had never seen before. Those people were very gracious and planned a great feast in Rabbit's honor. When the time for the feast came, Rabbit wore his fanciest clothes and a very strange hat that had four sticks, covered with pitch, sticking out of the top. Everyone was dancing, and Rabbit danced too. As the dance continued, everyone got closer and closer to the sacred fire in the middle of the circle. All the dancers began to bow to the fire; lower, lower, and lower they bowed. All of a sudden as Rabbit bowed very low, the sticks in his hat caught fire and bright flames glowed about his head.

The People were furious that someone would even think of touching the sacred fire. They became angry at Rabbit and chased him from their village, trying to catch him. But Rabbit, as you know, is a terrific runner, and very fast. He ran to the great water and jumped in, careful to keep his head above the waves. Those people couldn't follow Rabbit across the water, and so he escaped. This is how Rabbit tricked fire away from those people and brought it back for everyone.

TOO CLEVER

Sometimes animals could be too clever for their own good. Certain animals, like Coyote, were never satisfied with things and were always trying to improve their lot. Coyote never could leave well enough alone. In the desert Southwest, Coyote is always up to something.

The Pima remember the time when Bluebird was not blue but an ugly color.

AT THIS TIME, there was a lake. No river flowed in or out of it. It was in this lake that Bluebird bathed four mornings in a row while singing a song:

"There lies the place,
the blue water place.
I bathed in that water.
Now I am blue too!"

And so it was, he turned
the most beautiful color
blue you have ever seen.

Sandal-sole gorget carving of an animal with the umbilical cord still attached. Gorgets of this type, usually undecorated, were characteristic of the Northern woodlands Glacial Kame people. Like the stories about Coyote, even his image is sometimes problematic, hard to determine, and tough to pin down. The animal depicted on the shell pendant may be a coyote. Or it may be a mountain lion. Or a bear. Maybe it depends on the story you want to tell.

Now all this time, Coyote had been watching Bluebird, and he was hungry, but too afraid to go into the water to catch him. But when Coyote saw how beautiful Bluebird was now, he forgot his hunger and only wanted to be blue himself. So he asked Bluebird how he did it. Well, Bluebird was a nice fellow and told Coyote to go into the water four times and to sing this special song. Coyote did as Bluebird instructed him, and he became blue also!

Oh, now Coyote was truly proud. As he walked along, he looked one way, then another, to make sure everyone was watching him and admiring him. He started watching his shadow to see if it had become blue too. He was not watching where he was going. Coyote ran into a tree so hard that he was thrown to the ground. When he got up, he was the color of dust and dirt, and he has remained that way ever since. ☀

Trickster stories—like the story of Bluebird and Coyote—often warn about the problems of pride. Being clever is a good thing, but becoming too pleased with oneself can lead to trouble. Coyote has always been like this. Sometimes, Coyote plays tricks on other animals. And sometimes, those same tricks get played right back on him.

Wildcat Gets a New Face
(Ute)

Oh, back then, Wildcat didn't look quite as he does today. A long time ago, Wildcat had a long tail and long nose as well. Wildcat liked to sleep, and one day, he was napping on a rock. Coyote saw him there, and while Wildcat was snoring, Coyote walked right up and pushed in his nose and tail. Coyote went home pretty pleased with himself. When Wildcat woke up, he knew right away that something was wrong, and he knew that it was all Coyote's fault. So Wildcat went looking for him.

After a long day of playing tricks on people, Coyote had himself become tired and had lain down for a nap. At this time, Coyote had a short nose, and a short tail as well. Well, when Wildcat found him, he pulled that nose way out, and then did the same to Coyote's tail. Wildcat ran home, pretty pleased with himself. This is how Coyote's nose and tail came to be as they are.

WATCHING AND LEARNING

There are subtle lessons to be learned from the creatures with whom we share this world. Native people have always known that each creature has its own wisdom and have shared in that wisdom by watching carefully, by studying animals and the ways they interact with one another and their environments. Native American tribes have learned about their lands by seeing the world through the eyes of their relatives, through the eyes of the animal people.

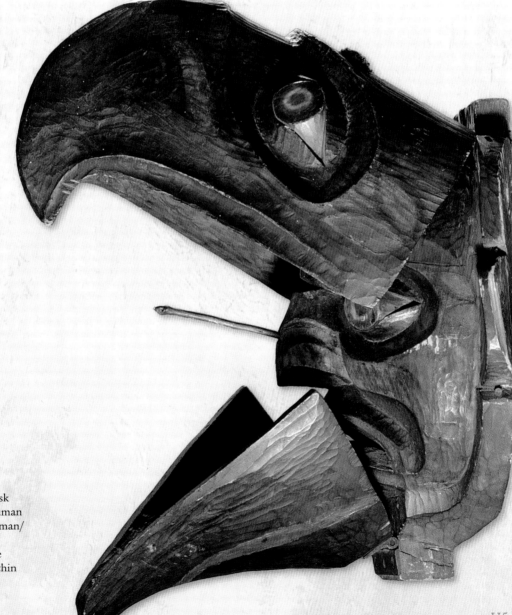

This Haida thunderbird mask (shown opened) reveals a human face, expressing the dual human/ animal nature of the spirits. Spirits within spirits. People within animals. Animals within people.

Cosmic Hands by Linda Lomahaftewa (Hopi/Choctaw), 1978.

CHAPTER EIGHT

Signs of the Ancient Ones

Hieroglyph

At the foot of a desert mountain
earth color beige, brown
tears in the
sand
darker
where water
meets dust
and ash
the drawings
left behind in dust take shape
form of love
and remembrance of those
left behind.
Following in the footsteps of a soul wound
a fragment
of memory
like water droplets pooling in dust
remaining like a desert pearl
then fading slowly, like the drawings in

dust:
panther,
wolf,
a spider's web,
remnants of the following
the delicacy and determination
leaving behind
to be studied
only when they look down
but who looks down at dust and ash?
Only the wounded
whose souls cry out
silent spaces of words
against stone
desert beige
and the backs of the dwelling places
long gone
and left
behind.

Enduring signs and messages are sent down from the past, and they are wonderful mysteries. In many parts of America, out among the hills or canyons or deep forests, carvings upon rocks can still be found. Who made them? And why? Were they meant for everyone to see? Or is finding them now a kind of trespassing on the conversations of the Ancient Ones? Can these signs and symbols still speak? Images, memories, stories, and objects all carry the past into the present. As we think about these messages from the past, we might wonder, too, about what kind of signs we are leaving for the future. How will our children's children know of us? What markers of our passing do we leave upon the land? Some of these signs, because of the material they're made from, or the care taken in making them, may last longer than others and have different stories to tell.

WINTER COUNTS AND BIRCH BARK

Among the tribes of the Plains—the Lakota, Cheyenne, Kiowa, and others—special hides were kept and used like calendars. These Winter Count hides were usually made of buffalo skin and kept a running account of the most important events observed by the tribe. All kinds of information was recorded: successful hunts, wars, and battles; deaths of important people; diseases; and the arrival of foreigners. Often wonderful or terrible events were recorded to represent a given year: celestial appearances, magical ceremonies, or the arrival of frightening new diseases.

These events were painted on the smooth side of the hide and were kept and added to from one generation to the next. Often during winter, the Winter Count hides would be brought out, and stories told about the events they recorded.

Among Native peoples who travel frequently, objects that commemorate important events, such as successful hunts, would be made small enough to carry—like this Inuit incised bow handle. Such objects may also have been carried to help insure the success of future expeditions.

Other tribes kept similar calendars and histories, but recorded them on different materials. Arctic people, like the Inuit, would carve pictures on bone or ivory to remember hunting expeditions, tragedies, or wars.

Tribes of the Great Lakes region, such as the Anishinabe people, make scrolls of birch bark, while ancestors of the Anishinabe also carved images upon the rocks. The sacred scrolls and stones record symbols relating to their Seven Fires Prophecy. This prophecy contains important tribal history that tells of the seven periods and places of their tribe's migrations. The wisdom contained in these prophecies continues to guide the lives of Anishinabe people to this day.

Plains Indian painted buffalo hide, used to record important tribal events.

In this way, many Native American tribes note the passing of years not numerically, but by recording and remembering important events and ideas symbolically. These objects (a hide, a scroll, a carving) would become keepers of the tribe's memory. And by looking at the images they preserved, storytellers, medicine people, and tribal leaders could recite detailed histories and beliefs stretching far back into the past. Many of these accounts have not survived, because they were made of material that decayed easily. Many stories may have been lost in this way.

Yet the materials used to record tribal memories are themselves important, and can be found in myth. Among the Anishinabe, birch bark was considered a special gift.

IT IS SAID THAT LONG AGO, Nenaboozhoo (the "spirit uncle" of the Anishinabe) was making arrows and was in need of feathers. "Only feathers from the offspring of the thunderbirds will do," his grandmother told him. "You must seek them in the place where clouds begin."

And so Nenaboozhoo climbed to the tallest mountains he could find and finally, after many days, discovered a nest with young thunderbirds. Clever, clever he was then and he changed himself into a rabbit so the thunderbirds would carry him up to the nest, thinking he was dinner for their children. So the thunderbirds carried him up to the nest, and there Nenaboozhoo remained as the days passed.

A long time Nenaboozhoo lived in the nest, abused by the children of the thunderbirds. They pushed him and pulled him, they pecked at his face, his eyes. Finally, Nenaboozhoo had enough. One day when the thunderbird parents were away hunting, he changed back to himself again. He killed the young thunderbirds and pulled their feathers from them.

Holding tightly to the hard-won feathers, Nenaboozhoo ran and ran, over hills, past woods, along the river. Finding their children dead, the thunderbirds flew after Nenaboozhoo in a fury. Lightning boiled up from their beaks and shot from

their eyes. Sheet lightning flew from the tips of their wings as they swooped down on him. Just as they were about to catch him in their claws, Nenaboozhoo saw a hollow birch log and leaped inside. Time and again the thunderbirds grasped and tore at the log, trying to rip it open with their talons. Finally, they relented and returned to their home in the sky. Nenaboozhoo waited a long time before coming out of that log! But when he did, he announced to everyone that the birch tree was a great protector of the People, and would always be a help to them and aid them in their lives. Then, in remembrance of the sharp talons of the thunderbirds, Nenaboozhoo made incisions on the birch bark so no one would forget his ordeal. But the original marks made on the birch by the thunderbirds also endured. Those marks look like their children, so that people will never forget their sacrifice.

WORDS THAT LAST

Rocks have been here a long time. It takes a lot to wear them down. Hundreds, even thousands of years later, we can still see the same surface of the stone that the ancient people saw. Signs left on these stones appear as if they were carved only yesterday, even though a thousand years have flown their shadows across the surface of the rock. Through these symbols, the past speaks and reaches out to us.

Imagine wandering deep into a red-rock canyon. All around are pictures and images, some carved, others painted on the faces of the rocks and upon the canyon walls. Walking quickly by them, the images appear to move and blur as shadows pass over them; yet they are silent. But if looked upon slowly, carefully, and closely, the stones may speak.

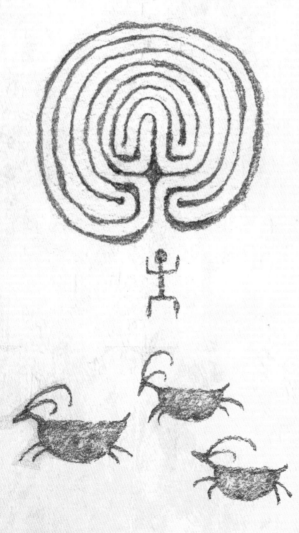

A Maze

This is a road of life. Mazes have been carved upon the rock's face to remind us that we are moving, always making our way. Just as the ancient people emerged from another world into this one, we are, all of us, threading our way through life's journey. At the center of the maze is death, which we may seem to avoid by turning this way and that, but eventually, if the nature of the path is accepted, death is peacefully acknowledged and harmony is restored.

Mountain Sheep

Hunger and power are the same. These images may have been used in magical ceremonies to help bring game animals to the People. Carving their images on the rocks might call the sheep to this place. It was respectful to honor the animals in this way before the hunt. So many of them! The hunt will go well. The People will not starve.

People of Power

Medicine people or spirits? Is there a difference? Here are signatures of people who speak through magic. Were they born here, among the rocks? Or did they enter the world through a small hole in the canyon wall? These images are seen high above the canyon floor. How did they come to be placed so high on the canyon wall? Did the person who painted them know the secrets of flight? The Sun-Headed Man has often wandered among these stones; long ago, he was generous with his small, fringed bag of pollen, placing his marks upon the rocks where he stopped to rest. Yellow ochre still adorns the stones.

Spirals

Such images may represent sipapuni, or "places where the People emerged from the earth." Does the spiral mark a place where this has happened? Or does it tell of the memory of such an event? Some spirals, at special times of the year, are marked by passing shadows. In this way the solstices, the stations of the sun, are remembered and celebrated.

Shield

A marker of a great battle? Or was this carved upon the stone to protect this place from prying eyes? Several shields can still be seen upon the rocks, each one unique. Often, people are seen wearing their shields. Was this for protection or because the shield's design says something about them? Is there a hidden language in the shield's decoration?

Water and Clouds

Water is life. Places of water had to be remembered. High in the hills surrounding this canyon, springs may be flowing, but how will you find them? Signs and maps upon the rocks may hint at their location. People have also used water signs and cloud signs to mark the places where their clans have paused or camped or lived. Perhaps carving clouds upon the rocks is a way of asking the clouds to journey to that place.

Corn

A living prayer? A loving portrait of that which gives life to the People? Such a symbol can mean many things at once: a charm, emergence from the lower world, a clan sign—or perhaps it was simply carved as a way to pass the time while resting after the harvest.

Badger

Badger is a great friend to the People. He knows the hidden trackways of the ground and has shown people where the healthful plants and their roots may be found. For this reason, he is to be honored. A thousand years have passed, and his image has not faded from the surface of the stone. But he is rarely seen above the ground, and because of this, his tracks are inscribed far more often than his portrait.

Sun, Moon, and Stars

Sometimes the things people see the most are also the things most sacred to them. Why were the symbols and motions of the skies recorded in stone? The ancient people watched the skies carefully, for the sky and the land are

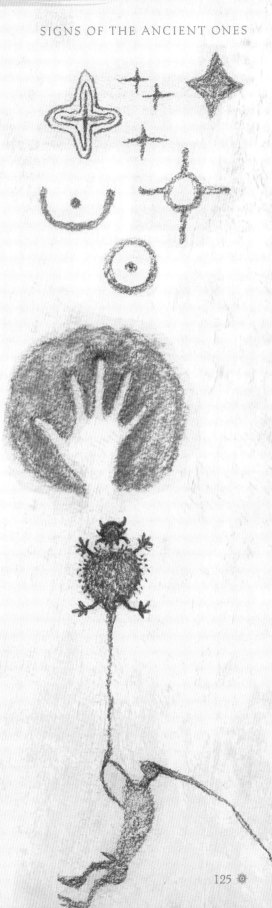

closely related. Movements of the sun and moon helped people track their year and were vital to knowledge of planting and harvesting. But the sun, moon, and stars were also people, with their own stories to tell. Here, on the rocks, are signs of a time when Sun walked this canyon and Stars were remembered as our extended family, as relatives of Earth Surface People. And Moon, didn't she rise just there, beyond the rock, above the river?

Handprint

These signs are the most frequently seen of all. Why? They might be signatures of living people; a way of saying: "Look!" "See!" "I was here, I lived upon this land." "I have stories to tell you of my journey." "Will you listen?" These signs upon the stones are there to remind us of all the ancient people who walked here before us, who built their houses among these canyons, who are, even now, watching us from the spirit world.

It is said that long ago, the young men used to hang down the cliffs from ropes woven from yucca. The medicine men would instruct them to do this and teach them about the animals and other forms they would paint on the rock. All these things were put on the rocks to remember them: stars, bear, badger, antelope, clan signs, spirit forms, spirals, the mark of their own hands. Stories, instructions, warnings, maps. Some say these marks were made a long time ago. Others say the spirits put those drawings there, that they put their marks upon the stones and watch over them still. Maybe both are true.

Satellite dish with wedding basket design by Hazel Merritt (Navajo), 1991.

CHAPTER NINE

Mythmaking in the Twenty-first Century

Beautyway

Nighttime.
The birds sing for the new dawn
in the skies falling ash
like snow over from the
fires above
lost angels.
We can no longer
force the stars to speak
our names
so we will call upon
the fires in midwinter
to tell the stories
stolen from the mouths
of seven generations to come,
of the days when ash rained
like falling fire

and we were able
to sing them home
with our rage,
our crying,
our calling the dawn,
in a world in
which the sun
lives in a red sky,
a house made
of daylight stars
and
rain.

We have encountered many stories from Native America, from creation stories to stories of help; listened to healing ceremonies, as well as heard tales of ghosts and spirits from other worlds; and learned how the animals received their names, and how animals and people live together and learn from one another. Some of these stories sound like they took place long ago and far away. But if you listen again, they could also take place in modern times as well.

Stories in the modern world can take many forms. Poems, songs, chants, ceremonies, but the best stories told today still derive from an oral tradition that continues to flow under every word, keeping the story's roots alive. Here we have a story that is told out of a Choctaw song, telling us about Nashoba, the wolf, a very tricky character, much like Coyote.

Nashoba, the Wolf

Nashoba, the wolf, was hungry.

Now, as far as wolves go,
they are handsome creatures,
and *Nashoba* was by far,
the most handsome of all.
His fur was sleek, black,
shiny in the sun,
so shiny his beauty would
blind all who looked at him.

And if there were those
who weren't blinded by the light
(and there weren't many)
Nashoba could flash the
most beautiful,
charming,
and handsome smile,

and then those
whose eyesight remained
would close their eyes
from such beauty,
and when they opened,
could not see again,
the last image of
Nashoba, the wolf,
and his smile,
pressed upon their eyelids.

Nashoba, the wolf,
although good-looking,
was hungry.
Just a little hungry.
The kind of hungry
that begins with a little sound
in the pit of your belly.
Gurgle, gurgle.
A tiny sound.
Not enough to really make a big stink,
but enough for the most
handsome wolf of all
to notice the rumblings going on.
"Hmmm," *Nashoba, the wolf,*
thought to himself,
"I'm a little hungry.
I think I'll go hunt rabbits."
So *Nashoba, the wolf,*
stood, shaking his beautiful
black coat that gleamed and

Mississippian carved shell head, early ninth century. Many contemporary Southeastern Native artists are looking to ancient ancestral artifacts for inspiration in creating beautiful new works, always with an eye to the past.

129 ☀

shone in the sun,

stood, and walked down the road.

That little gurgle, the one that begins

in the pit of your belly,

was becoming enough to make

a big stink.

Well, *Nashoba's* gurgle was

growing louder and louder.

GURGLE GURGLE GURGLE

"Oh," *Nashoba* said, starting to make a stink,

"I am s o o o o hungry.

I am s o o o o hungry."

GURGLE GURGLE GURGLE

"Oh," *Nashoba*, the wolf, moaned.

"I am so hungry."

Looking down, he saw some big gray rocks.

So he went over

to those rocks,

and opened his jaws wide,

you could almost see down his

mouth, into his throat,

past his tonsils,

GURGLE GURGLE GURGLE

and into his empty belly.

He opened his jaws wide, went up

to those rocks,

and stopped.

"Hmmmm," *Nashoba* said,

"If I eat those rocks, they'll just

cut up my belly,

tear up my
esophagus,
and boy will they hurt coming out.
Suk chuffa chugme honkah.
I am hungry.
I should hunt some rabbits."

It was a beautiful day.
Sunny and warm, unusual for
that part of the redwood forest.
Nashoba, *the wolf*, he walked along the road,
but he couldn't see the sunshine
pouring down from between
green needles and
around red bark.
Oh, that sound . . .
it was s o o o o o o loud!
GURRRRRGGGGLE
ROWWRROWWWWRRR . . .
"Ooooooohhhhhh!"
Nashoba moaned,
really starting to make a BIG stink.
He looked and looked,
no rabbits anywhere,
just big, wide, beautiful trees.
"Ooooooooohhhhhhhhhhhh,"
moaned *Nashoba*,
"I am so hungry, I could eat this redwood tree."

Calusa carved wolf's head, Key Marco, Florida.

And that handsome wolf, he opened his jaws wide,

you could almost see down his

mouth, into his throat,

past his tonsils,

GURRRGLE

GURRRRGLE

GURRRRRRGLE

and into his empty belly.

He opened his jaws wide, went up

to that beautiful redwood tree,

and stopped.

"Ooooh, I am so hungry," he said.

"But if I ate that redwood tree,

the bark would splinter in my insides,

tear up my gut,

and on the way out,

now that would hurt some.

Oh, I am so hungry,

Suk chuffa chugme honkah . . .

I should go hunt some rabbits."

Now, this is a story

that takes place in the here and now.

In the midst of these rocks,

these beautiful redwood trees,

are people, and their big,

beautiful houses.

Our friend *Nashoba*, he loves people.

He loves their gardens and

their chickens and

everything else in between.

Nashoba, the wolf,

that handsomest of all the four-leggeds,

was getting v e r r r r r r r y y y y y y hungry.

GGGGUUUURRRRRGGGLLLLE
GGGGGGUUUURRRRRRRGGLLLE
GGGGGGGUUUUURRRRRRRRRR
GGGGGGGGGGGGGGGLLLLE
RRRRRRROWWWWRRRRRRRR
RRRROWWWWWRRRRRRRRRR
RRRRROOOOOOOWWWWWWW
RRRRRRRRRRRRRRRRRR

"Oooooooohhhhhhhhhhhhhhhhhhhhhh . . ." he moaned,

"I am s o o o o o o hungry, I could eat that house over there . . ."

He was still looking good, still handsome,

but the hunger was making him weak.

He loped on over to the house,

checking his stride just to make sure he looked good,

and when he got to the house,

he opened his jaws wide,

you could almost see down his

mouth, into his throat,

past his tonsils,

and then stopped.

"Oh, I am s o hungry

GURRRRRGGGGLE

but if I ate this house, the bricks would turn

into mortar,

cut up my esophagus,

and boy that would hurt

coming out the other end.
I better go hunt some rabbits . . ."

Nashoba, the wolf,
by now was verrrrrrrrrrrrryyyyyyyyyy hungry.

GURGLE GURGLE

"Oh," he said to himself,
"I am so hungry . . . I don't think I can make it . . ."
And he collapsed on the ground.
But something tickled his nose,
and he opened one big, golden eye.
He had fallen at a big, beautiful open meadow with tall,
green grass.
And what do you think lives in
beautiful fields of tall green grass?

You guessed it—rabbits.
So *Nashoba*, the wolf,
after looking hard at those rocks,

at those redwood trees,
and at people's houses,
sang this song.

"Suk chuffa chugme honkah
Suk chuffa chugme honkah
Suk chuffa chugme, suk chuffa chugme
Eenpa so na tah ha."
"Awatale chukfe honkah
Awatale chukfe honkah
Awatale chukfe, awatale chukfe
Nashoba siya honkah."

"I'm a little hungry today,
I'm a little hungry today.
I think I'll go hunt some rabbits
To eat.

"I think I'll hunt some rabbits,
I think I'll hunt some rabbits,
Hunting rabbits, hunting rabbits,
I am Wolf."

And that's just what he did.

Nashoba, the wolf,
wasn't hungry
anymore.

A ceremonial club used in the Wolf dance, from the Nootka people, Northwest coast. Why are wolves primarily depicted with their mouths open? Perhaps it is because they are always hungry and talking, talking, talking!

Whether new or ancient, stories can have a timeless quality about them, and the moment they are told and retold by new generations, they take on a new life. Remember the power of words and the power of names? Remember how words can be magic? The words on the written page are powerful as well, and in retelling these stories we have given them life once again. The words, the stories, connect us to the past, and carry us into the future as we speak the words of the animal spirits and the old storytellers, bringing new life into the old words.

So, even now, Nashoba, the wolf, is prowling around the margins.

In Native American traditions, the whole world is a storehouse of wisdom. This wisdom is there to be appreciated by people who are willing to look for it and listen to it, whether they live in an apartment building or on a high desert mesa. All things in the world have a story and a spirit: people, animals, trees, rocks, seasons, everything in nature, everything created in beauty. Everything has power and is deserving of respect. When we stop long enough to

☀ hear the wind,
☀ watch and learn from animals,
☀ wonder about a beautiful object,
☀ listen to stories,
☀ gaze upon the ancient signs
  on a canyon wall,
☀ care for the earth,
☀ honor ancestors and family
  members,
☀ live well alongside our neighbors,
☀ respect the People who have lived longest
  on the land,

we are honoring that wisdom and the People who carry it.

ABOVE: Every rock has a story. This one lies on the Malpais lava flow, which Navajo tradition tells was formed from the blood of a slain giant.

OPPOSITE: Revered by many local people—Hispanic, Native, and Anglo-Americans—the shrine of El Tiradito in downtown Tucson, Arizona, is evidence that the sacred is all around us, even in the midst of urban sprawl. Photograph *El Tiradito* by Stu Jenks, 1996.

Coyote Girl by L. Frank (Tongva/Ajachumen), 1998.

A Word from the Los Angeles River

We are all storytellers, so we all have to be careful of what we say. Remember the phrase "I take it back!" usually after someone has said something unkind? The unkind words take on a life of their own, and once they have been spoken, they can never be taken back. That's why we have to be careful of the words we say and the words we write.

Stories are like that. Once spoken, they take on a life of their own. They change with the telling, but the essence, the heart of the story remains. Like when you were young and played the telephone game? It was always funny to see what the original story was and how it changed with each retelling. Sometimes the story changed a lot; but the basic sense of the story, or some of its sound, was still there if we listened hard.

We both grew up in Southern California, in a world surrounded by change, growth, and concrete and cars and things that some don't normally associate with the natural world. Growing up, we always thought that the Los Angeles River wasn't a real river: How can a river that runs in a concrete channel be real? Like everything else in this place, it seemed created by humankind. It was part of our sense of place but it was concrete. Human-made. Not a real river.

Not until many years later did we realize that the river was a real river; that it flooded in the rainy season of winter and slowed to a trickle in the hot, dry summer. The river likes to move and change, like most things in the natural world. When Los Angeles was being settled in the early part of the 1900s, the river liked to move around and flood folks out. So the Army Corps of Engineers came up with a flood-control plan that included forcing the river to stay sedentary in a concrete washway, not allowing her the freedom she was accustomed to.

Los Angeles River by John Humble, 2001.

Stories are told to bring us closer to the past. For native peoples, stories make connections between landscape, family, neighbors, ancestors, animals, and future generations. We forget so easily, but stories can bring the forgotten things home. Yet the stories we need the most, like the river, are sometimes forced to change course and, like water, sometimes go underground for a time, appearing to be lost themselves. Sometimes we grow up far away from where our ancestors were born out from the earth and so forget or leave behind the stories we once needed to know. Sometimes we even grow up with good stories, but lay them aside as we grow older. Yet the spirits of place follow us and the spirits of new lands find us, taking up important places in our lives. Sometimes the stories are just waiting, waiting to be picked up and remembered, waiting to be called back from the shadows. The Old Ones who live in the land still have something to say, still need to be acknowledged and respected. The Los Angeles River is no exception. We met the river again, very recently.

IT WAS NOT YET WINTER when we first spotted her, when we saw her coming down from the mountain and onto the desert plain, moving past ruined shopping carts, rusted metal, and flapping plastic, traveling along the concrete washway of the swollen river.

Still strong, the old woman picked her way slowly along the banks, following the narrows and traces of jimson, river oak, and nonflowering alata. She pored over the aspects of wet earth as if studying a map. She gazed at the trash, too—shards of glass or asphalt or steel—trying to make sense of the abandoned fragments of this new world.

Woven basket, Jemez Pueblo. New Mexico.

Her world was slowly dying, and she knew it. So using memories of the grinding of acorns, the boiling of sap, and the pulling of tule grass between teeth, she stretched the threads of anything she could remember from the old times and wove a round basket with dark diamond patterns. Blood from her fingers set her own story into it, into a form that might carry her memories for just a little longer. Over and over she filled and emptied the basket with water, wetting and softening the brittle grasses as she worked them.

The old woman tied in everything she could remember of her long road: her birth at the headwaters, the winding path out of the mountains, the sight of far-off places, the coming of the Spanish, the rise of the missions, the hard fate of being forced into obedience by men who didn't want the Old Ones around anymore. As she worked her nimble fingers around and around the basket, a hard wind rose up. On the quickening air she could smell the fires heralding fall, taste dust, and feel the anger rising in households as the devil winds came broiling down the desert sky and into the city—all signs of a hard season coming. She sang a song for the waters, for the weaving of stories, for the People who lived and died imprisoned by concrete walls. She dropped tobacco in the man-made washway. Then the rains came.

We hadn't been looking for her, really, we were just out walking, breathing the twilight air and sitting at the edge of the water, watching it lap against its concrete embankments. Looking up, we watched the city lights dance above the old woman's head and saw the haze of October hanging in the air. There had been hints and whispers of rain the night before, but these were blown away by fires in the hills and the hot wind that followed their flames. Now it began to lightly rain again.

As the rain fell and the old woman meandered past where we sat, we glanced down, seeing only the sparkles and stars of mica embedded in the stone sidewalk. Watching the old woman again, we had not noticed at first the two black eyes peering from below the dusk. Coyote had come upon our resting place, watching us from among the waving reeds that grow along the river out of cracks in the washway. We imagined what might be held in the old woman's basket of tule grass: a story of this place before the People came, before the concrete, before the cars? A story whose song sounded like rain falling among the reeds?

Coyote and the old woman knew each other well. Coyote and the old woman had lived together since the first days: two Old Ones who'd bucked the odds and survived it all. Old Man and Old Woman carrying on, complaining at each other through the long nights. Two spirits so much older than the city that sprang up around them. Two that managed to hold on. We wanted to know their secret, wanted to spend the whole winter listening to their tales. We just had to remember how to listen.

What story could we tell you that would make you understand this river a little more? What could we tell you, friend, that would make you want to know her, know her ways? Perhaps you already know something of the river, can remember some thread of a threadbare tale. Her power is still heard in the small things, the small voices that remain on the land, the small voices of the spirits of the Old Ones, whose stories can still be sought and found if you look and listen.

Such stories don't die but remain hidden in the background of a thousand distractions. They are carried by the voices still singing above the din of traffic and cars and horns and exhaust. They are the songs of the stars, the wind, the trees that burn in late summer and are reborn from the black earth of spring. They are found in the enduring voices of the People buried in the hills, in the pueblos, below concrete, glass, and asphalt. The storytellers still run in the hills, laugh in the alleyways, live in little houses along the freeways, in all the sacred places hidden below wherever our feet fall on this continent. They are the People who have lived to tell the tale and survived on bear grass, bottle glass, jimsonweed, wild alata, concrete, prayers, songs, corn, and chili burgers from Tommy's. They are the People still living in this land of death and glittering rebirth, this place where people come to be reborn and become ageless. Through story and song and respect, we can learn what we need to know to live on this land.

Watching the old woman wander on with the coming of evening, Coyote opens his mouth and speaks: "When the rain arrives, I come in from town, pick my way along the alleys, loping down the concrete channel, singing the song of the Western world. The few who can hear me come to the water, dropping alata and making their own songs in languages that most folk think faded with their dreams of a frontier." He paused, seeming to wait for applause, but then turned on all fours and sauntered back to town.

Later that night as we listened to the rain continue to fall, winding its way down the gutters to the river, we heard Coyote howling again. Heard him say, laughing, "I, I, I am like the river, like Old Woman and her children and grandchildren, I am still here!"

We both grew up along the Los Angeles River.
The river taught us many things.
The most important thing we learned
    was to just listen
        to what she had to say. ✳

Los Angeles River by John Humble, 2001.

Acknowledgments

Ari and Carolyn would especially like to thank Howard Reeves of Abrams Books for his support and perceptive comments on the text; Michael Karlin and Honorah Foah and the Mythic Imagination Institute for temenos; Clint Burhans for exceptional last-minute photography; Muriel Nellis and her team at Literary and Creative Artists, Inc.; and Robert Gould who believed in making this book happen.

Carolyn would like to gratefully acknowledge the storytelling traditions of Native America and the storytellers who see those traditions preserved every day, especially her husband, James Anderson, for the gift of a good story at least two or three times daily. To Paula Gunn Allen, Carole Lewis, Georgiana Sanchez, John Moreno, Susan Diaz, Patricia Estrada, Julian Lang, Nancy Richardson Steele, Maggie Steele, Cindi Alvitre, Gayle Ross, Kenneth Johnson, Joy Harjo, and my uncle, Philip Linscomb, *yakoke*. There is always a good tale or more there as well.

Ari would like to express his particular gratitude to his wife, Kris, for time and to his son, Robin, for many walks in the woods wherein he taught his father how place-names work; to Jay Stauss, Mary Jo Tippeconnic Fox, Michelle Grijalva, and the American Indian Studies faculty at the University of Arizona for granting me the honor of their friendship and providing invaluable assistance and encouragement during my studies. Special thanks to Mike and Monica Rao, Pam Gates, Gary Shapiro, Marcy Taylor, and Central Michigan University's English Department, College of Humanities and Social and Behavioral Sciences, and the President's Office for their enthusiastic support of my work, and to colleagues Jan Dressel and Susan Stan for their helpful comments on an early draft of the book. And to Scott Momaday, who taught me the magic of words, strongly encouraged this book, and taught me how to drive a Range Rover with my knees while eating a Blake's Double Meat Lotta-Burger. And to the storytellers themselves who gifted their words to the world long ago and still: Thank you.

List of Tribes & Nations Mentioned

A note on source material: Most of the information in this list was taken directly from tribal Web sites and tribally sanctioned written and published material.

*When discussing American Indian groups, it is important to note that we use the following terms when referring to groups of people. A **tribe** is a group of people who are bound by language, culture, religion, political governance, and community ties. A **band** is a smaller, often autonomous, group within a larger group or tribe. A **confederacy** is a larger group made up of smaller bands who work together for a common interest, often a political interest. When we speak of **nations** within American Indian communities, we are acknowledging the sovereignty status of these tribes in that they follow their own constitution, political governing body, and judicial body.*

Achumawi: One of eleven bands of Pit River Indians living still in their ancestral homelands in northwestern California, from Mt. Shasta to Mt. Lassen and throughout the Warner Range outside of modern-day Redding, California, and surrounding areas, including Burney, Alturas, and Susanville.

Alabama: Now known as the Alabama-Coushatta, this tribe merged with a band of Coushatta Indians in the late 1800s and resides currently in east Texas. Originally, they inhabited parts of what is now Florida, Louisiana, Oklahoma, Alabama, and Texas. Linguistically related to the other Muskogean tribes including the Koastati, Creek, and Choctaw.

Arapaho: One of the tribes of the northern Plains region, the Arapaho are culturally related to the Cheyenne and linguistically related to other Algonquian tribes. Split into two bands, Northern Arapaho and Southern Arapaho, they live now in modern-day Oklahoma (Southern band) and Wyoming (Northern band).

Blackfeet: The Blackfoot Confederacy consists of four bands of tribes that resided originally in the United States and Canada in the northern Plains. These bands are Pikuni/Peigan, North Peigan Pikuni, Blood/Kainai, and Blackfoot/Siksika. They currently reside in present-day Montana in the United States and Alberta, Canada. Their language is Algonquian and the language, like many other native languages, continues to evolve over time.

Cherokee: A confederacy of southeastern tribes linguistically related to the Iroquois or Haudenosaunee and culturally related to the Creek, Seminole, Choctaw, Chickasaw, and other southeastern tribes. The Cherokee migrated from the northeastern Haudenosaunee and moved south into parts of present day North Carolina, South Carolina, Georgia, Kentucky, Virginia, Alabama, and Mississippi. There are three federally recognized bands of Cherokee living in present-day Oklahoma and North Carolina: the Cherokee Nation of Oklahoma, the Keetowah Band, and the Eastern Band in North Carolina.

Cheyenne: A Plains region group of Algonquian speakers who are linguistically as well as culturally related to the Arapaho. There are two bands of federally recognized Cheyenne today: the Northern Cheyenne in Montana and the Southern Cheyenne in Oklahoma. The name Cheyenne actually comes from a Sioux and French word for the Cree tribe.

Chickasaw: A Muskogean tribe closely related culturally and linguistically to the Choctaw, and also culturally related to the other so-called Five Civilized Tribes. Originally a smaller Muskogean band from northern Mississippi and Louisiana, and parts of Alabama and Kentucky, the Chickasaw were removed from their ancestral homelands on the Trail of Tears and reside near present-day Ada, Oklahoma.

Choctaw: A loosely knit confederation of Muskogean people originally inhabiting parts of Mississippi, Louisiana, Alabama, and eastern Texas. One of the so-called Five Civilized Tribes forced on the Trail of Tears, the Choctaw were originally an agricultural people, and there are several federally recognized bands living in Mississippi, Oklahoma, and Louisiana.

Comanche: Once part of the Shoshone bands, the Comanche migrated around the year 1600 from Wyoming to parts of southeastern Colorado, southwestern Kansas, western Oklahoma, and northern Texas. As a southern Plains tribe, they are linguistically related to the Shoshone, Paiute, and Ute tribes and are culturally related to the Cheyenne, Kiowa, and Arapaho. A federally recognized band lives near Lawton, Oklahoma, today.

Coos: A confederation of tribes that still reside in south central Oregon and along the southern coast of Oregon. Primarily made of three bands: Coos, Lower Umpqua, and Siuslaw. Culturally related to the Klamath and Siletz Indians.

Cree: A tribe made up of many bands living in Ontario, Quebec, Saskatchewan, Manitoba, and Alberta, Canada, and Montana in the United States. An Algonquian tribe, they are culturally related to other northern Plains tribes in the United States and the Ojibwe in both Canada and the United States. The name Cree comes from the shortened Kristineaux, a name given to them by French traders in the 1600s. The Cree language is Canada's most widely spoken indigenous language.

Creek (Muskogee): A Muskogean-speaking confederation of tribes originally inhabiting parts of Georgia and Alabama, culturally related to the Cherokee, Choctaw, and Chickasaw and closely related culturally and linguistically to the Seminole. The name Creek was given to them by the English, and the word the Creeks use is Muskogee in English, *Mvskoke* in Muskogee. Two federally recognized bands live in Oklahoma and Alabama.

Crow: A Siouan-speaking tribe originally from the Yellowstone Valley in Montana. Culturally related to the Hidatsa and Mandan tribes, the Crow are considered part of the Plains Indian cultures. They reside near south central Montana near Billings at the Crow Agency.

The Five Civilized Tribes: A name given to the Cherokee, Creek, Seminole, Choctaw, and Chickasaw Nations by non-Indians to distinguish these nations from other Indians during the late eighteenth century. Because some citizens of these tribes assimilated early on into American society (such as by turning farms into plantations and owning slaves), they were considered "civilized" by the American government. The term is still used today.

Gallinomero: A southern band of Pomo Indians living near the Russian River in northwestern California. Culturally related to the Miwok and Yukots.

Great Lakes or Woodland Region: The region of peoples east of the Mississippi River, north of Cape Hatteras, north of the Great Lakes, extending along the St. Lawrence River to the Canadian Maritimes. These cultures include the Ojibwe, Huron, Miqmaq, Ottawa, Potawatomi, Menominee, Cree, Sauk, Fox, Kickapoo, Miami, Peoria, Illinois, Shawnee, Piankashaw, Prairie Potawatomi, Penobscot, Passamaquoddy, Mohegan, Pequot, Seneca, Cayuga, Onondaga, Oneida, Mohawk, Susquehannock, Erie, Conestoga, and Lenni Lenape (Delaware).

Hopi: One of the Pueblo tribes residing in northeastern Arizona near Black Mesa. They are Uto-Aztecan language speakers as well as (in the village of Hano) Tewa speakers who migrated north to First Mesa and maintain a separate cultural identity from other Tewa speakers.

Inuit: *Inuit* is a general term for a group of culturally similar indigenous peoples inhabiting the Arctic coasts of Alaska, the eastern islands of the Canadian Arctic, Labrador, and the ice-free coasts of Greenland.

Iroquois (Haudenosaunee): Made up of tribes including the Mohawk, Cayuga, Seneca, Onondaga, and Oneida, the Iroquois Confederacy lived in what is now New York State, along the St. Lawrence River. The United States borrowed heavily from the Iroquois Confederacy's system of governance to design the Constitution. Linguistically related to the Cherokee and the Erie Indians.

Kiowa: An Aztec-Tanoan–speaking tribe, linguistically related to the Tanoan-speaking Pueblo people in New Mexico. Culturally related to other southern Plains tribes, the Kiowa resided originally in parts of Texas, New Mexico, and Oklahoma; today the nation resides in Oklahoma.

Lakota: One of the seven Siouan-speaking bands of culturally and linguistically related Great Sioux Nation. The Lakota are the western branch of the tribe, also called Teton, and reside in both North

Dakota and South Dakota. The seven branches of the Lakota are Brule (Rosebud), Oglala (Pine Ridge), Sans Arcs (Cheyenne River), Hunkpapa (Standing Rock and Cheyenne River), Minneconjou, Blackfoot, and Two Kettle (Cheyenne River).

Malecite (Maliseet): An Algonquian-speaking nation that lives near New Brunswick, Canada, and belongs to the Wabanaki Confederacy, which includes the Miqmaq, Abenaki, Passamaquoddy, and Penobscot. A band currently lives in northern Maine.

Miqmaq (Mi'kmaq): The Mi'kmaq language, *Míkmawísimk*, is an Algonquian language spoken by 8,000 Indians in the Canadian Maritimes (particularly Nova Scotia) and a few U.S. communities. Their original term for themselves was *Lnu'k* (or *L'nu'k*)—"the People." *Mi'kmaq* comes from a word in their own language meaning "my friends"; it is the preferred tribal name now, though fluent speakers often use the adjectival form, *Mi'kmaw*. Variously spelled Mi'kmaq, Míkmaq, Mikmak, Mi'gmak, or Mikmaq.

Montagnais: Montagnais Innu is an Algonquian language spoken by about 9,000 people in eastern Canada. The Montagnais and Naskapi are actually part of the same Indian nation, calling themselves Innu. Their languages, however, have diverged enough that most linguists consider them separate languages (though some do class Naskapi as a dialect of Montagnais, or both as dialects of the Cree language). They are culturally related to the Cree.

Natchez: Muskogean-speaking peoples who originally inhabited parts of Mississippi and Louisiana; eventually due to illness and war assimilated into the Cherokee, Creek, Catawba, and Chickasaw communities in the southeast. There are some Natchez who live within the Creek Nation in Oklahoma today.

Navajo, or Diné: A large nation that extends into parts of Arizona, New Mexico, and southern Utah, the Navajo are perhaps one of the most well-known tribes outside of Indian country. An Athabaskan-speaking nation, *Dinétah*—or Navajoland, as they refer to the reservation—is the largest reservation in the United States.

Northern Paiute: A tribe whose language family is Uto-Aztecan and whose bands still live in northeastern California, Nevada, and southern Oregon. The Northern Paiute are culturally and linguistically related to the Shoshone. Their language, interestingly enough, is not related to the Southern Paiute dialect.

Northwest Coast: A cultural grouping of the many native nations who live in the Pacific northwestern United States and Canada, including the Bella Coola, Chehalis, Chemakum, Chimakuan, Chinook, Clallam, Coeur d'Alene, Columbia Salish, Colville Okanagan, Gitskan, Haida, Haisla, Halkomelem, Heiltsuk (Bella Bella), Kalispel, Kutenai (Kootenay), Kwakiutl, Kwakwala, Lummi, Lushootseed, Makah,

Nass, Nishga, Nitinaht, Nootka, Oowekyala, Puget Salish, Quileute, Quinault, Salishan, Sechelt, Shuswap, Siletz, Snohomish, Spokane, Squamish, Straits Salish, Thompson, Tillamook, Tsimshian, Twana, Wakashan, Wishram.

Ojibwe: Also known as Anishinabe, an Algonquian-speaking nation made up of 160 bands in Canada and thirty bands in the United States, they are culturally related to the Cree, Blackfoot, Cheyenne, Fox, Menominee, Potawatomi, and Shawnee. They currently reside from the Great Lakes region to Montana, and in the Canadian Prairie from eastern Quebec to western British Columbia.

Pawnee: A Caddoan-speaking confederacy of bands that includes the Chaui (Grand Pawnee), Kitkehahki (Republican Pawnee), Pitahauerat (Tappage Pawnee), and Skidi (Wolf Pawnee). Sometimes considered part of the Plains Indian cultures, the Pawnee traditionally are more culturally related to Southeastern tribes in that they were matrilineal and raised crops such as corn.

Pima: The Pima, also called Akimel O'odham, inhabited areas near the Salt River, Gila River, Yaqui River, and Sonora River in southern Arizona and northern Mexico. Currently, they reside in three communities: the Salt River–Maricopa and Gila River communities that they share with the Maricopa Indians; and the Ak-chin community, which is primarily made up of their close relatives, the Tohono O'odham, all in Arizona. Their language is of Uto-Aztecan origin.

Plains Indians culture: The Great Plains is the broad expanse of land that lies east of the Rocky Mountains in the United States and Canada. Covering all or parts of the states of Colorado, Kansas, Montana, Nebraska, New Mexico, North Dakota, Oklahoma, South Dakota, Texas, and Wyoming, as well as the Canadian provinces of Alberta, Manitoba and Saskatchewan, it is known in Canada as the Canadian Prairie. The Plains Indian cultures, made up of groups from Blackfeet, Crow, Sioux, Cheyenne, Arapaho, Comanche, Shoshone, and Kiowa, subsisted on the buffalo or bison. The buffalo roamed the western plains of the American mainland for tens of thousands of years, numbering in the millions until the coming of white hunters to the Great Plains, and thus were omnipresent in the natives' lives. The Indians used every part of the buffalo—hides, bones, internal organs. Some tribes also use parts (such as the skull) in religious ceremonies. Today, these cultures still exist in the parts of the United States typically associated with the northern and southern Plains.

Pueblo: The Pueblo speak languages of at least two different families. Languages of the Tanoan branch of the Aztec-Tanoan linguistic family are spoken at eleven pueblos, including Taos, Isleta, Jemez, San Juan, San Ildefonso, and the Hopi pueblo of Hano. Languages of the Keresan branch of the Hokan-Siouan linguistic family also are limited to Pueblo people: Western Keresan—spoken at Acoma and Laguna—and Eastern Keresan at San Felipe, Santa Ana, Sia, Cochiti, and Santo Domingo. The Hopi language, which belongs to the Uto-Aztecan branch of the Aztec-Tanoan linguistic family, is spoken at all Hopi pueblos except Hano. The Zuni language is connected with Tanoan.

Seminole: A Muskogean tribe culturally and linguistically related to the Muskogee Creek, there are Seminole tribes in Florida and in Oklahoma. They speak both Muskogee, which is the Creek language, and Mikkosukee, which is related to but different from Muskogee. The Seminole are known for their colorful patchwork. Several other bands live among the Seminole, including the Yamasee, Yuchi, and Apalachee.

Shoshone: A Uto-Aztecan tribe, living in parts of California, Nevada, Wyoming, Idaho, and Utah. Divided into regional bands known as the Eastern, Western, and Northern Shoshone, they are linguistically and culturally related to the Paiutes, Utes, and Comanche.

Skagit: A Salishan-speaking tribe living in western Washington state along the Skagit and Stillaguamish Rivers.

Tohono O'odham: A Uto-Aztecan language–speaking tribe in southern Arizona and northern Mexico, closely linguistically and culturally related to the Pima, or Akimel O'odham. The Tohono O'odham are also known to the United States government as the Papago, a term that the Tohono themselves rarely use anymore.

Ute: The Ute Indians, of the Shoshone Indian linguistic stock, were originally divided into seven nomadic and forest-dwelling tribes that lived on vast territory in Colorado and parts of Utah and northern New Mexico prior to the arrival of the European settlers; they were the Capote, the Mouache, the Parianucs, the Tabeguache, the Uintah, the Weeminuche, and the Yampa. Ute, which means "land of the sun" also gave the state of Utah its name.

Wichita: A Caddoan-speaking southern Plains tribe, linguistically and culturally related to the Pawnee. Their traditional land base included parts of Texas all the way up to southern Kansas. The Wichita currently reside near Anadarko, Oklahoma, with the Wichita-affiliated tribes Keechi, Waco, Tawakonie, Caddo, and Delaware.

Winnebago: A Siouan-speaking nation, linguistically and culturally related to the Iowa, Oto, and Missouri tribes and more distantly to the Dakota. Also known as Ho-Chunk, there are two federally recognized bands, the Ho-Chunk Nation of Wisconsin and the Winnebago Tribe of Nebraska.

Yaudanchi (from California): One of the original inhabitants of the San Joaquin Valley in central California, the Yaudanchi are a band of Yokut Indians who live now on the Tule River Reservation near Porterville, California.

Select Bibliography

Bierhorst, John. *Mythology of the Lenape: Guide and Texts*. Tucson: University of Arizona Press, 1995.

Boas, Franz. *Introduction to Handbook of American Indian Languages*. Lincoln and London: University of Nebraska Press, 1991.

———. Kathlamet Texts. *Bureau of American Ethnology Bulletin*, no. 26. Washington: United States Government Printing Office, 1901.

———. Tsimshian Texts. *Bureau of American Ethnology Bulletin*, no. 27. Washington: United States Government Printing Office, 1902.

Clark, Ella E. *Indian Legends from the Northern Rockies*. Norman and London: University of Oklahoma Press, 1988.

Cushing, Frank Hamilton. *Zuni Folk Tales*. Tucson and London: University of Arizona Press, 1992.

Dorsey, George A. *The Mythology of the Wichita*. Norman and London: University of Oklahoma Press, 1995.

Erdoes, Richard, and Alfonso Ortiz, eds. *American Indian Myths and Legends*. New York: Pantheon Books, 1984.

Evers, Larry, and Felipe S. Molina. *Yaqui Deer Songs, Maso Bwikam: A Native American Poetry*. Tucson: Suntracks and University of Arizona Press, 1990.

Giddings, Ruth Warner. *Yaqui Myths and Legends*. Tucson and London: University of Arizona Press, 1993.

Gifford, Edward W., and Gwendoline Harris Block, eds. *Californian Indian Nights*. Lincoln and London: University of Nebraska Press, 1990.

Gill, Sam D., and Irene F. Sullivan. *Dictionary of Native American Mythology*. New York and Oxford: Oxford University Press, 1994.

Grinnell, George Bird. *Pawnee Hero Stories and Folk-Tales*. Lincoln and London: University of Nebraska Press, 1990.

Judson, Katharine Berry, ed. *Myths and Legends of California and the Old Southwest*. Lincoln and London: University of Nebraska Press, 1994.

Lowie, Robert H. *Myths and Traditions of the Crow Indians*. Lincoln and London: University of Nebraska Press, 1993.

Merriam, C. Hart, ed. *The Dawn of the World: Myths and Tales of the Miwok Indians of California*. Lincoln and London: University of Nebraska Press, 1993.

Millman, Lawrence, ed. *A Kayak Full of Ghosts: Eskimo Tales*. Santa Barbara: Capra Press, 1987.

———. *Wolverine Creates the World: Labrador Indian Tales*. Santa Barbara: Capra Press, 1993.

Mooney, James. *History, Myths, and Sacred Formulas of the Cherokees*. Ashville, North Carolina: Historical Images, 1992.

Mourning Dove (Humishuma). *Coyote Stories*. Lincoln and London: University of Nebraska Press, 1990.

O'Bryan, Aileen. *Navaho Indian Myths*. New York: Dover Publications, Inc., 1993.

Parker, Arthur C. *Seneca Myths and Folk Tales*. Lincoln and London: University of Nebraska Press, 1989.

Parks, Douglas R. *Myths and Traditions of the Arikara Indians*. Lincoln and London: University of Nebraska Press, 1996.

Shaw, Anna Moore. *Pima Indian Legends*. Tucson: University of Arizona Press, 1995.

Smithson, Carma Lee, and Robert C. Euler. *Havasupai Legends: Religion and Mythology of the Havasupai Indians of the Grand Canyon*. Salt Lake City: University of Utah Press, 1994.

Swanton, John R. *Myths and Tales of the Southeastern Indians*. Norman and London: University of Oklahoma Press, 1995.

Thompson, Stith, ed. *Tales of the North American Indians*. Bloomington: Indiana University Press, 1966.

Underhill, Ruth Murray. *Singing for Power: The Song Magic of the Papago Indians of Southern Arizona*. Tucson and London: University of Arizona Press, 1993.

Walker, Deward E. Jr. *Myths of Idaho Indians*. Moscow, Idaho: University of Idaho Press, 1980.

Wissler, Clark, and D. C. Duvall, trans. and ed. *Mythology of the Blackfoot Indians*. Lincoln and London: University of Nebraska Press, 1995.

Ziibiwing Center of Anishinabe Culture and Lifeways. *Kinoomaagewin Mzinigas* (Little Teaching Books 1–5). Ziibiwing Center of Anishinabe Culture and Lifeways, Saginaw Chippewa Tribe of Michigan.

A Note on Sources

With the exception of her poetry and several stories original to Carolyn Dunn, the stories in this book have been gathered from textual sources and retold. We were committed to using stories that had been in print (many a long while) in several sources/versions and that, while carefully recorded, would greatly benefit from sensitive retellings. Many of the stories were originally gathered in the early part of the last century and were strongly affected by the "accents" of their European and/or American collectors, thus taking them even further away from the poetics of the tribes who owned (and still own) and told them.

Our goal was to return some sense of poetry and orality to these stories while not diminishing Native American oral tradition further by taking any stories that we knew or have been told and putting them into print for the first time if they did not already exist in print. In this, we wish to follow the respectful admonition of the great Native American writer, scholar, and activist Vine Deloria, who asked that stories still existing only in the oral tradition remain there.

Illustration Credits

Cody, Wyoming, USA; **Page 34:** *Storyteller* by Rozanne Swentzell, 2000. Used by permission of the artist; **Page 36:** Werner Forman Archive/Field Museum of Natural History, Chicago, USA; **Page 38:** Werner Forman Archive/Schindler Collection, New York; **Page 39:** Werner Forman Archive/ Field Museum of Natural History, Chicago; **Page 40:** Werner Forman Archive; **Page 41:** Werner Forman Archive/Edmund Carpenter Collection; **Page 42:** *Creation Legend*, Tom Dorsey. Museum purchase, 1946.24. © 2007 The Philbrook Museum of Art, Inc., Tulsa, Oklahoma; **Page 45:** Werner Forman Archive/Jeffrey R. Myers Collection; **Page 48:** Werner Forman Archive/Field Museum of Natural History, Chicago; **Page 50:** Werner Forman Archive/Utah Museum of Natural History; **Page 51:** Werner Forman Archive; **Page 53:** Werner Forman Archive/Private Collection, London; **Page 54 (top):** Werner Forman Archive/ Museum of the American Indian, Heye Foundation, New York, USA; **Page 54 (bottom):** Werner Forman Archive/The Greenland Museum; **Page 55:** Werner Forman Archive/Phoebe Apperson Hearst Museum of Anthropology & Regents of University of California; **Page 56 (left):** Werner Forman Archive/Eugene Chesrow; **Page 56 (right) and front cover (center bottom):** Werner Forman Archive/Canadian Museum of Civilization; **Page 58:** Werner Forman Archive/ Schindler Collection, New York; **Page 59:** Werner Forman Archive/University of Tucson Museum, Arizona; **Page 60:** *Stone People of the Sweatlodge* by S. D. Nelson, 1995. Courtesy of the artist; **Page 62:** Werner Forman Archive/Plains Indian Museum, Buffalo Bill Historical Center, Cody, Wyoming, USA; **Page 63 (left):** Courtesy of Ari Berk and Carolyn Dunn; **Page 63 (right):** Werner Forman Archive/Private Collection; **Page 64:** Werner Forman Archive/Field Museum of

Natural History, Chicago; **Page 65:** Werner Forman Archive/Canadian Museum of Civilization; **Page 67:** Werner Forman Archive/ Glenbow Museum, Calgary, Alberta; **Page 68:** Werner Forman Archive/Museum of Anthropology & Ethnography Academy of Sciences, St. Petersburg; **Page 69 (left):** Werner Forman Archive/National Museum of the American Indian, New York; **Page 69 (right):** Werner Forman Archive/Museum fur Volkerkunde, Berlin; **Page 70:** Werner Forman Archive/Anchorage Historical & Fine Arts Museum, USA; **Page 71 (top):** Werner Forman Archive/Private Collection; **Page 71 (bottom):** Werner Forman Archive/Maxwell Museum of Anthropology, Albuquerque, NM, USA; **Page 72 (top):** Werner Forman Archive/Museum fur Volkerkunde, Berlin; **Page 72 (bottom):** Courtesy of Ari Berk and Carolyn Dunn; **Page 73:** Werner Forman Archive/Maxwell Museum of Anthro- pology Albuquerque, NM, USA; **Page 75:** Courtesy of Ari Berk and Carolyn Dunn; **Page 76:** Tony Abeyta (Navajo), "Gathering from Four Directions," 1999. Ranchos de Taos, New Mexico. Photo by R.A. Whiteside. Courtesy National Museum of the American Indian, Smithsonian Institution; **Page 78 (top):** Werner Forman Archive/University Museum, University of Alaska; **Page 78 (bottom):** Werner Forman Archive/Jeffrey R. Myers Collection; **Page 79:** Werner Forman Archive/Glenbow Museum, Calgary, Alberta; **Page 80:** Werner Forman Archive/C. Pohrt Coll., Plains Indian Museum B. Bill Hist. Center, Cody, Wyoming; **Page 82 (left):** Werner Forman Archive/Provincial Museum, Victoria, British Columbia, Canada; **Page 82 (right):** Werner Forman Archive/Provincial Museum, Victoria, British Columbia, Canada; **Page 83:** Werner Forman Archive/Museum of the

Index

Page numbers in *italic* indicate photographs or illustrations.